LIVING

in the

KNOW

The Adoptee's
Quick-Start Guide
to Finding Family
with DNA Testing

GERALDINE
BERGER

Byram Books

LIVING

in the

KNOW

Cover design by Erin Seaward-Hiatt

All graphics by Geraldine Berger unless otherwise credited

Interior formatting by Melissa Williams Design

Edited by Kimberly Caldwell-Steffen

Library of Congress Control Number: 2021904795

ISBN: 978-1-7367203-0-1 Paperback Edition

Printed and bound in the United States of America

First printing 2021

Published by Byram Books

ByramBooks.com

Visit www.geneticgenealogycoach.com

For my beloved parents,
Leonard Berger, MD, and Doris K. Berger, who have always lovingly
and courageously supported my journey to living in the know.
Dad, you are my constant—my North Star.
Mom, you and your memory live on forever in me.

For Stephen D. Yale, whose love, encouragement, and belief in me
is a constant source of joy and inspiration.
Stephen, you are my best friend, my light, my love.

When you go through a hard period,

When everything seems to oppose you,

. . . When you feel you cannot even bear one more minute,

NEVER GIVE UP!

Because it is the time and place that the course will divert!

—Rumi, The Essential Rumi

Contents

Foreword

ALMA (Adoptees' Liberty Movement Association/The ALMA Society), the pioneer nonprofit organization fighting for the rights of adoptees everywhere, was founded in 1971 by adoptee Florence Anna Fisher.

In 1973, Fisher authored The Search for Anna Fisher, the memoir of an adopted woman who dared to seek out the truth of her origins at a time when such behavior was socially unacceptable. Later that year, Readers' Digest Condensed Books published an abbreviated version of the book, which, as a result of Ms. Fisher's frequent appearances on radio and television and in countless newspaper and magazine articles, quickly spread the word about ALMA's work in reuniting families separated by adoption laws. ALMA's international mutual-consent adoption reunion registry is the oldest, most comprehensive and successful registry of its kind.

The adoption reform movement (to restore adoptees' rights to their own original birth information) quickly became part of many Americans' daily conversations, as the number of adopted persons in the United States was estimated to be near six million in the mid-1970s.

As the coordinator for ALMA, I receive new members' applications and have the wonderful opportunity of providing one-on-one service, working with them to provide instruction on how best to conduct their searches. Helping others find closure is a rewarding experience.

Author Gerri Berger and I have known one another for almost thirty years. She joined ALMA in 1991 and became a valuable resource in our nationwide network of search volunteers in the New York metro and Southern Connecticut regions. Gerri and her birth mother were reunited through ALMA's registry in 2007.

The use of DNA testing as a means of finding genetic relatives has exploded since test kits became commercially available. That has led to a field of study called *genetic genealogy*, in which professional genetic genealogists like Gerri Berger use DNA evidence to assist adoptees and others with unknown parentage by identifying their birth parents and unlocking the truth of their origins.

In 2014, Gerri aligned her passion with her livelihood. She has proven herself an expert, as time and time again, she has solved adoption search cases that were thought to be unsolvable.

One case in point is an ALMA member whose birth mother deliberately named someone other than the member's birth father on her original birth certificate. The adoptee tested with several DNA companies and eventually asked Gerri to take her case, though it seemed impossible without additional matches. Gerri knew firsthand how disappointed the adoptee was, as Gerri's search for her own birth father was fruitless for several years. So, unbeknown to the adoptee, Gerri continued intermittently working the case and never gave up.

One day, the adoptee received a voice message from Gerri out of the blue: she had solved the case. An obscure DNA cousin match had turned up, and Gerri had pursued the family and worked the case tenaciously until she was able to identify the adoptee's birth father and make contact with the family. That adoptee's case was one of the longest and most difficult in ALMA history.

I have been a member of ALMA since 1991, when I began searching for my own biological family members. With ALMA's guidance, I used the resources available at the time and was able to locate my biological mother, whom I had the opportunity to meet when I was fifty-five years old. But she passed on without providing me the name of my birth father.

About eight years ago, I DNA tested, and though I met maternal relatives, the testing didn't reveal any paternal biological relatives. Just two years ago, however, at the age of eighty-three, I finally received a paternal match. I contacted that person, but we were unable to solve the case. Then I asked Gerri for assistance, and within a matter of days, she contacted me to let me know that she had identified my biological father.

Unfortunately, my biological father had never married, and I found no biological siblings on that side. Gerri built my family tree, it is ever growing, and I am continuing to make contact with my biological relatives. None of this would have been possible without her analysis of my DNA results.

So many lives are touched by adoption, and so few know much about it or are misinformed. Gerri is passionate about reforming adoption law to restore adoptees' equality as citizens by granting them the right to their own original birth information. She is working to create awareness about discriminatory adoption laws that impact the lives of millions of adult American adoptees and their families. Her "Adoptee's Family Tree" illustrates just how many lives are touched by adoption in the United States.

This book is an excellent and much-needed resource in the adoption community. Gerri lights the way for adoptees and others with unknown parentage, who may not know that there is a path to *living in the know*. DNA testing is a game changer, placing the power to access the truth of one's origins back where it belongs—in the hands of the individual. Gerri is a beacon of hope for adoptees who are victims of a broken system and need the assistance of a professional genetic genealogist. Through her own story and the stories of others, she illustrates that there is power in knowing who you are and that living in the know is healing.

I highly recommend this book to those who are seeking expert guidance on how to get started on their journey or want to learn the basics of finding biological family via DNA testing. Helping others discover the truth of their origins is Gerri's true calling and passion. The profound importance of the work and the sensitivity with which she approaches adoptees, people with unknown parentage, and family members cannot be overestimated. It is literally life changing.

I often tell Gerri to work her magic, as we have been teaming up to solve cases for years—our favorite words are "Case closed!" But it is not magic; it's years of experience and tenacity.

I am one among many adoptees who is eternally grateful to Gerri for helping me to discover fully the truth of my origins. It has made all the difference in my life.

Here's wishing you success on *your* journey to living in the know!

—Marie H. Anderson
ALMA coordinator

Introduction

Welcome and thank you for choosing this book. I hope it will help you or someone you love on the journey to *living in the know*.

I am a New York adoptee and a professional genetic genealogist, who helps adoptees and others with unknown parentage to identify and locate their birth parents and other members of their *families of origin* (aka "birth families"). I am also an adoptee-rights activist.

The purpose of this book is to guide others on their journey to living in the know. I want you to get to know me, and I invite you to join my Facebook group, accessible from my website, www.geneticgenealogycoach.com, so that I can get to know you and hear your stories.

TWO SETS OF PARENTS—SO MANY NAMES

As adoptees, we have two sets of parents—the ones who made us and the ones who raised us. Each set has uniquely contributed to who we are, and all of them are our *real* parents. This is simply a reality, though people from each set sometimes argue the point.

In this book, I refer to the biological (aka "first," "birth," "natural," "genetic") parents and other family members as "birth parents," "biological father or mother," and "families of origin." I refer to adoptive or foster parents and other members of those families as "adoptive mother or father," "adoptive family," "foster parents," and "foster family."

While these terms have been commonly used in the mainstream for decades, some birth mothers take offense to the term "birth mother" and prefer to be referred to as their child's "mother" or "first mother." The terms in this book are used solely to differentiate between adoptees' two sets of parents for the sake of clarity.

LEGISLATIVE OBSTACLES

As of the publication of this book, only ten states in the United States (Alabama, Alaska, Colorado, Hawaii, Kansas, Maine, New Hampshire, New York, Oregon, and Rhode Island) currently grant adult adoptees *unrestricted access* to their original birth certificates (OBCs). This means that upon request and for a nominal administrative fee, adoptees may obtain their OBCs, as is the case for all *nonadopted* adult citizens.

The remaining forty states and Washington, D.C. have some form of *restricted access*, placing numerous conditions on adult adoptees' ability to obtain their OBCs and/or the information on them. In some states, information is redacted prior to release of the OBC to the adoptee. The laws vary widely from state to state, and some are complex. Approximately half of these states require adoptees to petition the courts for their OBCs, and court orders are required to obtain them. The remaining half enforce other conditions—such as the adoptee's date of birth, consent of the birth parents, the redaction of birth parents' names, or the registration of all parties in a state-run mutual-consent registry. The bottom line is that not all adult adoptees in states with restricted access will be able to obtain their own OBCs—only those who meet the criteria for access under state law.

As a result of the current laws in these forty states and Washington, D.C., many adoptees have no idea who they are or where they come from—their original identities, parentage, ancestry, and heritage.

We are who we are in relationship to other people. As such, our original identities—the truth of our origins—involve the identities of our birth parents, as we are their sons and daughters. We are descendants of all of their ancestors. Genetically speaking, who *we* are is approximately 50 percent of who each of *they* (our biological parents) are.

No American citizen should be subjected to the humiliating experience of pleading with a court for his or her own original birth certificate. Being denied access to your own OBC and not having the same right to your birth information as all nonadopted citizens enjoy is demeaning, perpetually infantilizing, discriminatory, and a violation of your civil, constitutional, and basic human rights. This is the plight of millions of adult American adoptees.

WHAT IS LIVING IN THE KNOW?

Living in the know is actively living *with* knowledge versus without it. It is enlightenment versus ignorance and darkness.

Living in the know is also a choice, a journey, and a state of being. Insofar as one's original identity, parentage, origins, ancestry, and heritage are concerned, living in the know is a basic human right—it is one's birthright.

This book was written for adult adoptees and persons with

unknown parentage who have little or no knowledge of their original identity, parentage, family health history, ethnicity, and heritage, and who want to connect with biological family members and discover the truth of their origins. This book is for people who want to be free of the lifelong pain and preoccupation of *not knowing*. They want the inner peace that only such knowledge and self-knowledge can bring. They aspire to *live in the know*.

If you are reading this book, it is most likely because you are still searching for your birth parent(s) or other members of your families of origin. I have been where you are now. I was there for most of my life, so I intimately understand your plight. I was forty-two years old when my birth mother and I were reunited via ALMA and fifty-two years old when I identified my biological father via autosomal DNA testing and genetic genealogy.

For many of us, the search for the truth of our origins is frustrating, emotional, and deeply personal. My near-impossible searches for my own birth parents spanned a cumulative thirty-four years. Looking back, I realize that the struggle, difficulty, and pain of those searches were not the curses I believed them to be at the time. Rather, they were blessings that set me on the path I believe I was destined to take: guiding others to living in the know.

MY CREDO

I believe it is every human being's basic human right to know and have access to the truth of his or her origins, which is defined as *original identity*, *parentage*, *ancestry*, or *heritage*. And I believe this right supersedes any other individual's right to privacy. This is my credo. Why? Because is fundamentally right and fair. Period.

That conviction is widely shared around the world. Although the United States has not ratified the United Nations Convention on the Rights of the Child (UNCRC), 191 of the 193 member states of the United Nations *have* ratified it. The only other member state that has not ratified the UNCRC is Somalia. More on this in Chapter 7.

In alignment with my credo, I implore all nonadopted persons who have DNA tested to help adopted relatives by sharing your family tree information. Keep in mind that *your* family tree, to a varying extent, is also *their* family tree—only *they* have never seen it before. Imagine what that must be like.

Information as simple as the names of your parents, grandparents, and great-grandparents is a big help to adoptees. You don't have to know who the adoptee's birth parents are. In fact, in 99 percent of cases, you won't have any idea. Simply providing *your own* family tree information (ideally a pedigree chart linked to your DNA results) is a great start and may be enough information for a genetic genealogist like me to help an adoptee solve the mystery of his or her biological parentage. You will be giving your relative a great gift: help on their journey to living in the know.

Please be the person you would want your relative to be if you were in the adoptee's shoes—a humanitarian.

THE GOALS OF THIS BOOK

Living in the Know is not a textbook on genetic genealogy that will teach you how to become a genetic genealogist, nor does it strive to be that type of resource. It is a guide, a companion on your journey—a friend who knows the way and wants to bring you to living in the know. The primary goal of this book is to cut through all the information that's available on DNA testing and genetic genealogy and provide a *Quick-Start Guide* and my own proven strategy to launch you on your journey to living in the know.

I will describe my own journey, and some of my clients, whom I affectionately refer to as "my adoptees," will describe theirs. The work is personal. My adoptees confide to me everything they know about the circumstances of their births and adoptions, their feelings about their searches, their greatest hopes and fears, how their families are reacting to their searches, what is happening in their reunion processes, and how they feel about all of it. I listen, share aspects of my own journey, advise them, and coach them through possible search outcomes and the reunion process. I also serve as the intermediary between them and members of their families of origin.

Approximately 50 percent of my clients have struggled unsuccessfully with a search for their birth parents, with or without the help of well-meaning volunteers, before retaining me. The other 50 percent say they don't have the time or inclination or they just can't wrap their head around the search process, often because it is so emotionally charged for them.

What they all have in common is:

- They want and need a professional genetic genealogist who is committed to the work and specializes in cases of unknown parentage to solve their case.

- They want the help of an experienced intermediary who knows what to say and how to approach members of their families of origin to ensure the best possible first contact and reunion.

- They want to live in the know, and at this stage of their lives, they are ready to give themselves the gift of the truth of their origins by having someone with expertise do the work for them.

- They have had enough of lifelong wondering, fruitless searching, and the emotional roller-coaster of promise and disappointment. They're tired of it, they're ready to know *now*, and they don't want to go it alone anymore.

Search outcomes are as different as the people they involve. Through our stories, however, I hope adoptees and those with unknown parentage will realize that they are not alone, and I hope the nonadopted gain better insight into our experiences.

Last but not least, another goal of this book is to create social and political awareness. Many adoptees and others with unknown parentage have no idea there are people and organizations out there to support them on their journeys to living in the know. They have no idea whom to contact or how to get started. They may never have heard of the Adoption Reform Movement or know there are ways to get involved at the state level to change the laws that separate them from their families of origin or prevent them from accessing their own OBCs.

WHOM THIS BOOK IS FOR

This book is primarily for adoptees and others with unknown parentage who want to jump-start their search in the most efficient and effective way and read about the journeys of others like them. It is for the people who love them—their adoptive families, their children, their families of origin who may not yet know them, and those who want to help them on their journey to living in the know. This book is also for people or families who have surrendered children for adoption.

THE QUICKEST WAY TO START

Genetic genealogy is not for everyone; the learning curve is steep, and information is everchanging, as the technology in the field advances daily. This *Quick-Start Guide* is the first of its kind. It's meant to appeal to those who don't want to spend their free time for weeks, months, or years learning about the field of genetic genealogy in order to live in the know. This book is written in five parts and each part can be read independently of the other parts, insofar as prerequisite information or context is concerned.

If you are ready to dive into a search immediately, start with Part 4, "Your Journey to Living in the Know." After you have created your account on www.Ancestry.com and ordered your testing kit, you can read the other parts of the book in whatever order interests you. For more information or to contact me about your search, please visit my website, www.geneticgenealogycoach.com.

Whatever your reasons for choosing this book, I hope it will prove to be a beneficial resource. It is my hope that you will share it with other adoptees or persons with unknown parentage in your life. In so doing, you will be giving them something of deep meaning and importance—support and guidance on their journey to living in the know.

PART 1

Living in the Know

1

The Truth Seeker

> *In all of us there is a hunger, marrow-deep, to know our heritage—*
> *to know who we are and where we have come from.*
> *Without this enriching knowledge, there is a hallow yearning.*
> *No matter what our attainments in life, there is still a vacuum,*
> *an emptiness, and the most disquieting loneliness.*
>
> —Alex Haley

LIVING IN THE KNOW IS A CHOICE

Living in the know is a choice—the choice of the truth seeker. Truth seekers seek the truth not because they are unafraid of what they may find, but because it is their nature.

Truth seekers are born, not made. The nature of the truth seeker is such that he or she cannot bear *not knowing*.

If the truth seeker is an adoptee or a person with unknown parentage, living in the know is a quest, a lifelong preoccupation that extends far beyond basic curiosity. The truth seeker is inwardly compelled to search. For the truth seeker, there is no other choice—it is simply *what is*. As the truth seeker grows, living in the know becomes his solemn promise to himself, as much as it has always been his destiny.

The truth seeker cannot bear the darkness that exists in the recesses of her being, knowing that her own life began cloaked in secrets and lies and that the truth of her identity and heritage has been withheld from her—and will be forever more. She must discover the truth so she can free herself of the emotional prison inflicted by (a) the restrictive laws of the state in which she was born and adopted or (b) family members.

Sometimes an adoptee's adoptive parents are the ones with-holding information from the adoptee. Some adoptive parents never tell their adopted children that they were adopted, and the adoptee discovers the truth much later in life, either by finding the adoption papers among a parent's possessions after he or she passes away or via DNA testing. These folks are called *late-discovery adoptees* (LDAs). In cases of unknown parentage that do not involve adoption, it is most common for the individual to be raised by his biological mother, who never shares the truth of his paternity with him. In many cases, his mother is married with more than one child, and all of her children believe that her husband is their biological father, when in fact they have different fathers. She may have conceived one or more of them before, during, or after her marriage by a man other than her husband, who may or may not know that one or more of her children are not biologically his.

Some discover this truth in adulthood via DNA testing. Those believing they are full siblings—or others who may suspect they are not—will DNA test and discover that, in fact, they are half siblings.

If their mother is alive and confronted by her child(ren), she may refuse to reveal the identity of their biological father. Sometimes she doesn't know, or it's a toss-up between two or more men—which is so embarrassing for some women that they would rather be perceived as knowing but choosing not to say than reveal a list of possible biological fathers. About 20 percent to 25 percent of my clients are either LDAs or individuals with unknown paternity.

Whichever of these scenarios is the case, it troubles the truth seeker's soul that she lacks answers to basic questions, namely, "Who am I?" and "Where do I come from?" She does not just *want* to know; she has a burning, lifelong *need to know*. It is her quest—as it was mine.

What a cruel and unusual punishment to be stripped of one's true identity and ancestry at birth or in the earliest years of life, only to become an adult and learn that one also has been stripped of the right to access one's own birth information in perpetuity. It is identity theft of the most vicious kind. No human being should be discriminated against by having his birthright forever withheld for no reason other than he was not born within the construct of marriage (or because his own parents decided that he should never know).

It is unconscionable that in this day and age, forty states and Washington, D.C. (as of the publication of this book) still have laws in place that support this despicable and discriminatory practice.

For the truth seeker, it is a fate he cannot and will not accept. He must *do something* to change his fate.

No matter how well the adoptee is loved by his adoptive family, no matter how early in his life he was adopted, and, per Alex Haley, "no matter what [his] attainments in life," his need to discover the truth of his origins persists, as may his need to meet and get to know his genetic family members.

In the vast majority of cases, the truth seeker's search is *not* about finding other parents to replace the ones who raised him.

He loves his adoptive parents—they are his mom and dad and have been his whole life. He does not wish to hurt, insult, or abandon them or their lifetime of memories and experiences together as a family. He simply must know the truth of his origins. Some adoptees choose not to tell their adoptive parents of this need, for fear of hurting their feelings. Some choose to search only after their adoptive parents have passed away.

The exceptions are typically those who were raised in adoptive or foster families with abusive or otherwise dysfunctional parents. In these cases, the adoptee searches for members of her families of origin (most commonly, her birth mother) with the hope that she will be able to experience the love, kindness, and sense of belonging that was lacking in her adoptive or foster family.

These are basic human needs; we all want to be loved and treated kindly and to experience the feeling of belonging. It is also part of the human condition to seek fulfillment of those basic needs elsewhere when they are not being met at home. Though this is a far more common occurrence in romantic or spousal relationships than it is in parent-child relationships, it can exist there as well.

These are but two ends of the spectrum of what motivates adoptees to find their families of origin, and sometimes a combination of factors are involved. If I had to identify the motivator that most share in common, that's easy. They are truth seekers and can no longer tolerate what they call "the *not* knowing."

What is meant by "*the not knowing*" is not knowing who they look like in this world, who their birth parents are, why they were surrendered for adoption, whether or not their biological father knew about them, what their birth parents' relationship was, how they met and why they didn't stay together. It's not knowing whether or not their birth mother thinks of them, or ever tried to search for them, or wishes to know them, or will accept or reject them if she is alive and they are able to make contact with her. It's not knowing whether or not she wanted to keep them; or what she went through during her pregnancy, their birth, and thereafter. It's not knowing if she or the biological father is still alive. It's not knowing their family heath history or if they have full or half siblings and all the feelings that accompany those questions. There is much more—but generally, the adoptee's lifelong preoccupation with these questions (*our birthright*) and how it feels *not to know* the answers to them is what is meant by *"the not knowing."*

Are we all truth seekers? Is being a truth seeker part of the human condition that exists within all of us to varying degrees? I want to say yes, but I am not sure. I would like to think so. However, I have met adopted people who claimed to have no need or desire to know their families of origin or who claim they are only interested in family medical information. That seems unnatural to me, as I am an adoptee and I know what it feels like *not to know.* But again, each person is different.

Many adoptees, especially those born and adopted during the Baby Scoop Era (1945–1975), a period characterized by a record-high rate of premarital pregnancy, childbirth, and newborn adoption, have experienced being shamed for their need and desire to know—or at least their willingness to openly admit it. They are asked, "Haven't your parents been good to you?" or "Why would you want to hurt your parents like that after all they have done for you?" and other similar rhetorical questions. You know who the shamers are. Their tone of voice drips with disapproval and disdain. Their questions are intended to make you feel wrong, bad, ungrateful, or otherwise defective for wanting to *live in the know* while simultaneously

5

giving themselves a self-esteem boost. They believe themselves to be superior and their comments to be an act of loyalty to your adoptive family—the inference being that you *do not* have the same loyalty toward them, as evidenced by the fact that you expressed those needs and desires. I call this the Shame Game. Don't play it.

When you muster the courage to make yourself vulnerable to another by sharing your deepest truth, and the person you share it with shames you or otherwise uses it against you, walk away. That person is not capable of giving the support you deserve. Having never "walked a mile in your shoes," that person has no right to weigh in with self-righteous platitudes.

Since people operate from intention, you must always question the source of the shaming. Is the source a close family member or loved one who feels threatened by your need/desire to search for your roots? Is he a close friend of your adoptive parents or an adoptive parent himself? Those who truly love you and are capable of it will support you emotionally in your quest to discover the truth of your origins. Those who can't or won't support you clearly have their own agendas and their well-being, not yours, in mind. Ignore them. You trusted them and made yourself vulnerable, and their response was to shame you and poop on your dreams. Are they worthy of your time or attention any longer? Only you can answer that. Unfortunately, for many of us who were born in the 1940s, 1950s, 1960s, and 1970s, that ship has already sailed. Shamers did their damage when we were children—or at whatever time in our lives we began to verbalize our *need to know* to others.

The shamers were likely adults during the Baby Scoop Era, or they came to accept and adopt the beliefs of their parents, who were adults then. This mind-set began as a result of widely accepted assumptions (and the social sentiments about those assumptions) that formed during the time—and likely as a direct result—of many states opting to place adoptees' original birth records under permanent seal.

Prior to adoptees' birth records being placed under permanent seal, it was considered normal and natural for adoptees to want information about their birth families— the truth of their origins. After states sealed birth records, adoptees' need to know was deemed socially unacceptable and even considered to be abnormal. Many people believed that there was something wrong with an adoptee who had that need or that the adoption had failed—the couple and the adoptee were unable to create the ideal substitute for a biological family whose children were born to them naturally. These attitudes further reinforced the practice of secrecy, and ultimately, prevented adoptees from attempting to discover the truth of their origins.

Further, such adoptees were considered to be rejecting of their adoptive parents/families and ungrateful for having been adopted by them. This is absurd, predominately as those who adopted children (particularly during the Baby Scoop Era) were motivated by *their own* emotional and psychological needs and desires to become parents. They were seeking to form the traditional family unit that they were not able to create on their own, via childbirth. It had nothing to do with a saintly, selfless, charitable impulse to rescue a child being orphaned by a birth family for its own social and/or financial reasons.

For adoptive parents, the adoptee is *their* answered prayer. When the adoptee grows up and expresses her desire to know about her birth parents/families, the adoptive parents may *feel* rejected or slighted, as if their love and the life they provided to the child was not good enough. Essentially—and unfortunately—some come to believe that they failed their adopted child in some way. Such needs and desires are usually communicated before the age of legal majority, when the adoptee is just naturally curious and not even old enough or emotionally mature enough to consider that raising the questions or expressing the need and desire to know the truth of their origins may hurt their adoptive parents or threaten existing family bonds.

If adoptees are exposed to shamers at a young age, they have likely learned to respond to shaming comments with, "I'm only interested in searching to learn my family health history." Somehow, this response makes the adoptee's need and desire to search (and by extension, the adoptee himself) more palatable in the eyes of the shamers in his life. Some adoptees shame themselves out of their own need to know with similar self-talk because of these types of early experiences.

Of course, sometimes a question is simply that. Some people sincerely ask similar questions but with an open ear and an inquisitive, unaccusatory tone. They may be naturally curious and truly attempting to understand and empathize with your point of view. It may be difficult for them to imagine having the same need or desire if they were in your shoes. It's not always what you say; it's how you say it. Even young children pick up on the tone of the person with whom they are speaking.

All of this said, *it is not* an adoptee's responsibility to manage her parents' emotions, while repressing her own human need to know the truth of her origins. To expect her to do so is a form of emotional abuse that sends the message that the adoptee's needs and feelings don't matter as much (or at all) and that she should gladly be willing to forgo them to placate and protect the feelings of her adoptive parents.

It is the parents' job to see to the emotional needs of their child—not the other way around—except, of course, in the case of elder care by adult children, a situation in which the care-giving roles are reversed. This is not to say that adult adoptees cannot or should not be empathetic toward their adoptive parents. But adult adoptees can express their need to know, explain their motivations, and state clearly that it has nothing to do with wanting to replace their adoptive parents—nor does it have to do with the love, loyalty, and appreciation that they feel for them and always will, thereby assuring them that those bonds will never be broken. Even under those circumstances, some adoptive parents may have a negative emotional reaction, but again, it is not the adoptee's job to manage her parents' emotions or to allow her adoptive parents' reactions to deter her from what *she* needs. The adoptee is a person in his or her own right at any age and has feelings and needs that matter as much as anyone else's.

What is different about the adoptee is that he had no choice or active role in (a) the decision of his birth mother and/or her parents to place him for adoption and relinquish all parental rights or (b) the decision of his adoptive parents to adopt him. Even though he was an innocent pawn in the decisions of others, based on *their* collective needs, the adult adoptee often is expected to manage his adoptive parents' emotions as well as those of his birth mother, should he be able to locate and contact her. He asks himself, "How will my adoptive parents feel when I tell them that I need or want to know the identity of my birth parents?" and "How will my birth mother feel about my locating and contacting her? What if she never told her husband or children about me?"

While the adoptee is placing such care and concern around his parents' emotions to ensure they get what *they* need, who is doing that for *him*—the one who had *no choice* in the matter? Is he even doing that for himself? Does he not feel entitled to do so? What and how many experiences throughout his life, and with whom, may have contributed to his feeling (or belief) that others and *their* feelings and emotional needs are more important than his own? These are questions for all parties involved to consider.

Thankfully, my adoptive parents understood my need to know, and I was able to communicate my motivations and feelings to them clearly when I was in my early teens. They were willing, when I reached the age of eighteen, to help me achieve what I hoped to. I had their blessing. Also, thankfully, my birth mother and my biological father's family were open and welcoming. They were willing to share information and have a relationship with me as well as introduce me to their spouses, children, and other relatives. As you will see in other stories in Part 5, this is not the case for everyone. An adoptee who is stonewalled by her adoptive or birth parents (or both) often carries a heavy emotional toll—the feeling of being emotionally abandoned by both sets of parents, which can contribute to general feelings of worthlessness.

Many adoptees hide behind the desire for medical information, when the truth is that they need to know who they are and where they come from. Their family health history is an important and necessary part of that, but it is not the only motivation for their search.

When I am approached by adoptees hoping I will take on their searches, some add voluntarily, "I'm just searching because it's important to me to have family medical information."

I respond with, "You don't have to do that with me. I am an adoptee myself, so I understand *all* the reasons. Is that really the only motivation for your search?" This is where most breathe a sigh relief and begin to share that they have always wanted to know the circumstances preceding their birth and adoption—whom they look like and where they come from. They hope that their birth parents are still alive, will want to meet them, and will be willing to have a relationship with them. If it's likely that their birth parents have already passed, due to advanced age, they share their desire to know if they have full or half siblings, whom they would also like to know.

We are human. We want to be loved, and we want to be validated. We want to know (and hope it's true) that we were loved and that our lives meant something to our mothers who *surrendered* us for adoption. Many of us want to hear our birth mothers say, "I loved you then, and I love you still. I have often wondered about you and hoped that you were raised by parents who loved you as if you were their own flesh and blood. I'm glad you found me. I never wanted to give you away."

It's deep. It's emotional. It's private. And our deepest, darkest fear as adoptees or others with unknown parentage is that none of that is true—and that our need will never be met, for whatever reason. It is the child within that possesses this need. It is the unhealed part of the self that was traumatized by having been separated from our birth mother at birth, in infancy (aka the preverbal stage of development), or in early childhood.

Of course, some truth seekers really are only interested in their family health histories—though I have never encountered them in a professional capacity, only socially.

It is absolutely normal and natural to want to know who you are and where you come from. Further, the human brain does not like unanswered questions. It will attempt to answer the unanswered questions until there is resolution. If the answers cannot be found, the questions will persist within.

And the longer the questions burn, the more the search for the answers can become an obsession. This is also a normal and natural human psychological phenomenon.

Please, do not allow anyone to shame you out of living in the know. You cannot be shamed out of being human, nor should you be. Perhaps it would be appropriate for you to establish healthy boundaries and inform shamers when they cross them.

To truth seekers, closeted and otherwise, I hope this book will inspire and empower you to give yourself the gift of the truth of your origins, and that you, too, will experience living in the know.

LIVING IN THE KNOW IS A JOURNEY

Living in the know is a journey. It begins with the need and desire to discover the truth and the willingness to do something about it. Some people thought about searching years ago, but they never knew how to go about it and gave up. Some have concluded that now is the right time for them to search, but they don't know how to get started. Some have searched on and off for years, registered with adoption reunion registries, and may have even petitioned the court in the county in which they were adopted for a court order giving them access to their own birth information. Some have DNA tested but have gotten stuck, with or without the help of others. Many feel hopeless and believe that they have exhausted all possible avenues that may lead them to living in the know . . . or they don't even know that avenues exist.

Your journey to living in the know may be short and easy, or it may be long and arduous. It can be a joyride; an emotional rollercoaster; a nightmare, in that your greatest fears may be realized; or something in between. Your journey may include all of the aforementioned emotions at different stages. Everyone's journey is different, and there is no way to know, in advance, what yours will be like. But the truth seeker embarks on his journey anyway. He knows he can withstand whatever the journey will bring. What he can no longer withstand, however, is passively wishing or praying for the answers and self-knowledge that his soul so desperately craves. He can no longer stand the feeling of endless wonderment and disconnection from his own truth and heritage.

It has been said that when the pain of where one is exceeds the fear of the unknown, only then will most people act to change their circumstances. It takes courage to embark on this journey. Courage isn't the absence of fear; it's the willingness to act anyway. Some adoptees are paralyzed by their fear that their birth mothers will reject them. They already feel that they were rejected once, in infancy, because their mothers didn't keep them, even though most adoptees realize their birth mothers had no real choice then. Prior to contact with their birth mothers, adoptees often say they fear a *second rejection*, because it would be emotionally devastating for them to discover she doesn't want to know them at a time in her life when she *does* have a choice.

In the past, adopted children were often referred to as "unwanted children," and many of us were aware of that term growing up. In most cases, nothing could be further from the truth. Social conventions of the past mandated that young, unmarried women *surrender* their babies for adoption to protect the birth mother's reputation as a virgin before marriage, lest she be considered "damaged goods" or a social outcast. This practice was also thought to be in the child's best interest, to protect him from the stigma of illegitimacy, which was (and is still) accomplished via legalized identity theft called an *amended birth certificate*—a falsified birth record naming the adoptive parents as the child's birth parents—and his subsequent adoption.

The very term *surrender* is defined as "to cease resisting and to submit to authority or to give up or hand over a person, right, or thing, typically on demand." In most cases, there is nothing truly voluntary about the process. Needless to say, there are exceptions.

In the 1970s and earlier, the majority of young women signed away their children and their parental rights under duress, namely at their parents' insistence, in an effort to protect the young woman's reputation as well as their own. Some young mothers recount sobbing with grief as parents pushed them to sign relinquishment of parental rights forms that stated they were not signing under duress.

The "choice" they were often given was, "Keep the baby and move out—you're on your own." Or, "Place the child for adoption, come home, and never speak a word of this to anyone . . . ever." Some choice!

There was no *real* choice. A minor with a newborn and nowhere to live, no job, and no one to rely on could not care for her own baby, and she knew it. Neither of them would survive under those circumstances. She was "damned if she did and damned if she didn't."

That choice in and of itself was severe emotional abuse, from which many young mothers never recovered. Separation from their children, usually their first born, was an emotional scar they bore for life.

Young mothers were often shamed by their parents (and sometimes by the nuns or employees of unwed mothers' homes). To avoid the shaming, some young mothers would say they were attacked (date raped) in the hopes of eliciting pity versus punishment. This was one of the oldest stories in the book, though a small percentage of pregnancies did occur this way.

Young mothers were told not to be selfish (how's that for projection?) and that it was in the children's best interest that strangers raise their babies, because those strangers were older, married, and had more resources. They were told that the adopting parents would "give the child a better life," than they could. They were asked, "Don't you want your child to have a better life?"

In most cases, it would be more accurate to say that adoptees' maternal grandparents did not want to be the subject of community gossip and shaming brought on by having an unwed daughter with a newborn. Instead, they demanded that their daughter either leave with the infant or return home without him or her.

Is it any wonder that many of these young mothers never got over their anger toward their own parents and became pioneers of the Adoption Reform Movement? Is it any wonder that these women fought to open adoption records so that when their children reached legal majority age, they would be able to locate and reunite with their mothers?

In any case, the outcome was the same: the baby did not go home with the birth mother or her parents. The baby was referred to as *unwanted*. *Homeless* was more like it.

The grandparents' fear of what others would think or say about them or their daughter was the deciding factor in placing their own grandchild into the hands of strangers. Many birth mothers were minors and as such, one of their parents also was required to sign the relinquishment of parental rights.

Though every story is different, this process was the norm in the Baby Scoop Era. It may give you some idea of what your birth mother experienced before you were surrendered for adoption.

"Get Empowered and Go Spit!"

I encourage adoptees and others with unknown parentage who fear rejection to embark on the journey to living in the know. "Get empowered and go spit," I tell them, meaning take a DNA test and contact me when the results are in. I try to nudge these birds from the nests of their own fear, in the hopes that they will one day be free of "the not knowing." It's liberating whatever the outcome, and in most cases, their own worst fears *are just that*.

It can be a difficult emotional barrier to hurdle, but I remind them that they can always DNA test and choose not to make contact with their birth parents or other members of their families of origin. It's interesting to note that after getting over that hurdle, none of my adoptees has made the decision not to make contact. Not one—so far.

The truth seeker has always wanted to live in the know, has tried and failed, and has taken breaks on his journey as necessary acts of self-preservation and reprieve from the obsession to know his own truth. He is willing to get on the road again and knows he will, because it is his nature, but after twenty, thirty, forty or more years of fruitless searching, the very prospect of doing so again can seem like an exhausting act of futility. He declares, "I will find . . . I will be successful," and then the little voice inside his head says, "No you won't," based on his prior experience. I know because I've been there many times. My journey to living in the know spanned over three decades, during which time I evolved into a spiritual warrior.

LIVING IN THE KNOW IS A STATE OF BEING

Living in the know is a state of being. It is a feeling of liberation and freedom from the oppressive laws and/or family secrets of the past that stand between you and the truth of your heritage.

Living in the know is transformative and soul-strengthening. *There is power in knowing who you are.* You are *reconnected*, after a lifetime, to all who came before you. You have come home . . . to yourself. Suddenly, the whole of who you are makes sense at the deepest level, and a good deal of what you believed about yourself to be original—because you didn't share those things in common with your adoptive family—now has origins in your ancestors (parents, grandparents, great-grandparents, etc.). As it turns out, you're not *that* original . . . but it feels great. You are of this earth, through these bloodlines. You didn't fall out of the sky into a hospital nursery or your adoptive family's home. (Not that adoptees actually believe that; it's just that sometimes it *feels* that way.)

It's incredibly moving to be able to say, "I am . . . " and to know that *you are.* For example, "I am a *Mayflower* descendant."

Harking back to the idea that who we are is who we are *in relationship to other people*, it's amazing and a real paradigm shift—okay, that's an understatement . . . it's a minor earthquake—to discover in the middle of your life other parts of your identity that you never knew about. In essence, *everything* you've believed to be true about yourself is only a partial truth . . . and now there's all this other stuff about you that is also true.

It takes quite a while to shuffle these new cards into the deck of your reality and your whole identity. To hear information that's new to you, to hear someone else say it who has always known this about you, whereas you did not, and to understand that it's true and then to say it aloud for the first time is like trying on a costume and looking at yourself in the mirror, trying to process that *this* is part of who you are. It's weird.

As it turns out, I *am* a *Mayflower* descendant. How strange. My beloved sister Rohana (I have six maternal half siblings, two sisters and four brothers) was the first person to tell me so, on my forty-second birthday. What a priceless gift for someone like me—an adoptee. She gave me the gift of living in the know.

When I first heard this information, I flashed back to a fifth-grade Thanksgiving celebration at the Quaker Ridge School in Scarsdale, New York. All of the students and teachers were dressed like the Pilgrims. The boys were outside roasting turkeys and doing other manly things with our beloved gym teacher, whom everyone called *Gersh* . . . an abbreviation of his surname. The girls were inside in our respective classrooms, rolling out pie dough, wearing bonnets and aprons. It was a lot of fun. I remember thinking, with flour and Crisco under my fingernails, that *my* ancestors were Jews from Eastern Europe, and their lives were much different in 1620 . . . and they probably didn't make pies like this. Who would have guessed that I was actually a tenth great-granddaughter of John Alden and Priscilla Mullins and a direct descendant of twelve other *Mayflower* passengers? Certainly not I.

During one of our first conversations, in 2007, I remember telling my birth mother that I was having trouble reconciling my ancestors' identity with my own and that I didn't *feel like* I could be a descendant of theirs, based on what I knew about the Pilgrims and myself. She said, "Don't be fooled . . . they were *very rusty people*, my dear. They were told not to travel to the new world, that they would never make it, and they even if they did, they would never realize their dreams. And you know what they said?"

I was captivated. "What did they say?"

"They said, 'Oh yeah? Watch this!'" my birth mother said.

Suddenly, my opinion changed. That was *totally* me—since birth! *Now* I knew where my tenacity came from. I said aloud, "I am a *Mayflower* descendant." Yes. *Now*, it fit. That said, I'm also a descendant of other religions and cultures from other parts of the world.

Our tenth great-grandparents are twelve generations behind us, and each of us has 4,096 tenth great-grandparents. That's *a lot* of ancestors. John and Priscilla account for two of my 4,096, and I know who a few dozen others were, but that still leaves over 4,000 ancestors to discover, some in parts of the world where it's simply not possible due to the absence or inaccessibility of records. Some will be forever lost to time.

Living in the know is the gift that keeps on giving. It's not just about finding your birth parents. It's a never-ending journey of discovery and self-discovery. What begins as an effort to learn about your ancestors morphs into a journey of *self*-discovery, as you learn what parts of them echo in you. By the way, you don't have to be a person with unknown parentage to experience this. Just dig backward in your family tree and get to know some of those folks. They're "your peeps," and their stories are waiting to be discovered.

For adoptees and others with unknown parentage, finally knowing the truth in and of itself feels joyful and victorious . . . and a little surreal. It makes you wonder if you are dreaming and if it is really possible that your prayers have been heard and answered. You try to remember whether or not you actually made that deal with the devil at the crossroads—if only you could know the truth. You are now a believer in miracles, whereas before, miracles like this were something that only happened for other people. There is a buoyancy—an unmistakable *lightness of being* . . . a feeling of peace. It's dreamlike after a lifetime of experiences that led you to believe that you would never know. At last, you are living in the know.

This is the best way I can describe how it has been for me. It has been all that and more, as my journey continues to unfold fourteen years post-reunion. The feeling of living in the know is what makes my adoptees declare that I am their "friend forever," their "fairy godmother," and their "angel." Richard Cole, one of my adoptees, calls me "Madame Rue," a gypsy-with-a-crystal-ball character that he created in a fun fiction about his journey to living in the know. That one always makes me laugh!

Many of my adoptees and I become friends during their journey, and we keep in touch beyond the end of their search. They follow up with pictures, reunion stories, holiday and birthday greetings, and sometimes a question or two about how to handle a particular situation with a birth-family member after the honeymoon period has ended. I find it very moving, meaningful, and rewarding to be woven into the fabric of their lives in this way.

It is my hope that you will discover for yourself that the search for your birth parent(s) is just the first leg of your journey to living in the know. Pictures of your ancestors may surface, and you may see uncanny resemblances to your face in theirs, which is also a bit surreal after a lifetime of not even remotely resembling anyone in your adoptive family. You may have the opportunity to get to know some members of your families of origin and visit the homes and hometowns of your relatives. You may have the opportunity to learn about your ancestors through family stories, visit the places they lived, touch the things that they touched or made or built, and visit their final resting places. You may also begin to experience or recognize *synchronicity* in your life, for the first time.

It is an incredible experience when the things of your ancestors find their way into your hands—placed there by a close family member who you are only just getting to know.

It's also incredible when you realize that before you were living in the know, you had been inexplicably drawn to the places of your biological family members or ancestors (or both) or had been taken there by circumstances or events in your life. I have a long list of these experiences since being reunited with my families of origin.

Feeling the Juice

"Stomping the soil of your ancestors," as I call it, is something I recommend everyone do—not just adoptees or people with unknown parentage. It's not uncommon to have a visceral response to the land or the places they lived. To be there is as close as any of us can come to knowing what life was like for our ancestors. It's incredible. It feels like a homecoming . . . only you have never lived there.

On my first trip to Mendham, New Jersey, a town founded by my ancestor Ebenezer Byram, it felt more like I was *returning* than visiting for the first time. I likened it to the way I feel driving into Henniker, New Hampshire, the town where I went to college; I feel a sensation of connection to the place turning on inside me, somewhere between my heart and my solar plexus, when I'm about a mile from the center of town.

I have not felt this way in every location where my ancestors have lived—and I have certainly not been to them all. But there are a few places where I feel what I call the "juice," the stuff of spiritual connectedness and belonging. This is not to say that I feel I should live there—only that whenever I visit, I feel as though my ancestors have pulled me there by invitation. I experience it as feeling that they know I am on my way, they are welcoming me, and they are glad when I arrive. Sounds crazy, right?

That's okay—I'm good with it. It's very real for me, and it happens every time I visit there. I don't really think about it, but inevitably that feeling washes over me again about a mile outside the town. It's like an inner *knowing*. I am connecting/connected to them—and they are connecting/connected to me, and I feel very connected to that place.

I also felt the juice when I met my birth mother and six half siblings for the first time. With people versus places, it's moving, it's intense . . . and it's exhausting, in a good way. It's not dissimilar from the experience of falling in love. You're in a heightened state of awareness. The world seems brighter. Everything looks better, sounds better, smells better, tastes better, feels better. You are hyper-tuned in to the person (or people) and everything around you. You feel blessed. Your prayers have finally been answered. You feel more alive. You belong to each other. You're feeling the juice—the love, the connection—and it feels like you have known one another forever. Your souls recognize one another. It's unmistakable. The bond doesn't feel instant; it's gentler—more like an acknowledgment that the bond has simply always been. I hear of others having the same experience, and I see it in their reunion videos. This bond is why the hugs last for minutes. People hold each other and rock. They struggle to speak in complete sentences. They cry and hug some more. They're home.

I hope that you, too, will have the opportunity to experience the juice and what it feels like. No matter what happens or whether or not the relationships you hope for are possible, living in the know is life changing. Imagine what you will be free to do, create, and become without your lifelong preoccupation gnawing at you, usurping years of your time and energy. Living in the know is freedom and peace of mind; it's what inspired me to want to help you and others do the same.

2

The Truth Seeker Is a Spiritual Warrior

Ibecame acquainted with the term *spiritual warrior* in an article on Deepak Chopra's website.[1] Below, I have placed the qualities that define the spiritual warrior in bold, abbreviated the descriptions (apologies, Deepak), and added my own words relevant to the truth seeker and his search for the truth of his origins.

- The spiritual warrior is **aware** that he is at war with the darkness of secrets, lies (omissions are lies) and *the not knowing*.

- He has **courage** and continues on his path despite pain and—knowing that the prospect of living in the know is worth enduring the discomfort of the journey.

- He has **discipline** and knows there will be obstacles on the journey, but when those occur, he'll keep going when others would quit.

1—Adam Brady, "8 Traits of a Spiritual Warrior to Help You Combat Avidya," Chopra, accessed March 1, 2021, https://chopra.com/articles/8-traits-of-a-spiritual-warrior-to-help-you-combat-avidya.

- He is **relentless** and surrenders ego in favor of creating the space for *spirit* to enter.

- He is **self-aware** and **astute,** paying attention to his own thought traps so he can zoom out and course correct. In essence, he can get out of his own way.

- He is **patient** and knows that things happen on the Universe's timetable, not his own; he recognizes that there is a larger picture unfolding that he cannot yet see, but when the right moment arrives, he seizes the opportunity and takes the right action.

- He possesses **sweetness**—the Dalai Lama reminds us that "Compassion and tolerance are not a sign of weakness, but a sign of strength."

- To the spiritual warrior, **love** is all that is. It is the core of his being and all other beings. Expanding the field of love for himself and others is his ultimate goal. Love heals all wounds. It is that transformative power that can change the world. The spiritual warrior shines the light of his love into the darkness to transmute it into knowledge and healing.

All of my clients with unknown parentage are spiritual warriors, as I imagine you are, since you are reading this book. Each of them could write their own book about their journey to living in the know.

PART 2

My Journey to Living in the Know

3

Growing Up

Every journey is a long and winding road, and my journey to living in the know is no different. My journey is, in many ways, my life story, as it spanned most of my life and is ongoing.

I am or have been a daughter, granddaughter, sister, friend, student, athlete, musician, girlfriend, wife, doggie mom, aunt, search angel, corporate executive, adoptee rights activist and genetic genealogist (and many of these things at once, as we all wear many hats). Throughout those years and experiences, I was also an adoptee in search of the truth of her origins.

Life was and is the foreground of my experience. My experience and feelings around being an adoptee and my quest to live in the know were a part of my life, usually in the background but periodically moving in and out of the foreground. Attempting to separate the two, in life or in this book, is like trying to wash the spots off the leopard. The leopard and his spots are one . . . as is my long and winding road. The longing expressed in the melody and lyrics of "The Long and Winding Road," by Paul McCartney and John Lennon, always makes me think of my search for my birth mother.

'60s LOVE CHILD

"I am a 1960s love child." I love saying that—it sounds so *cool!* After all, the 1960s were a time of great social revolution in the United States. It was the time of John F. Kennedy, Lyndon B. Johnson, and Dr. Martin Luther King Jr. It was the time of the Civil Rights Movement, the Women's Liberation Movement, and the British Invasion by rock bands like the Beatles and the Rolling Stones. It was the time of the lava lamp, paper flowers, bell-bottom jeans, marshmallow shoes, tie-dyed T-shirts, experimental and hallucinogenic drugs, free love, Woodstock, the Vietnam War (and protest), long hair, peace signs, and the Apollo 11 lunar module *Eagle* landing on the moon.

During the 1960s, many mainstream American teens assimilated to the hippie culture, rebelled against traditional values, experimented with drugs, and participated in America's second sexual revolution (the first being in the 1920s). Oh, and abortion was illegal.

A *love child*, by definition, is a person who was conceived in a moment of passion between two people who were not married to one another, or one who was born out of wedlock, or was born of a romantic liaison. Anyway, *love child* sounds a lot more positive and a lot more fun than the more demeaning alternatives that, for millennia, have been a mainstream attempt to hack at the human wholeness, legitimacy, and goodness of babies who were not born within the construct of marriage. Imagine, an advanced society shaming newborns who had nothing to do with the circumstances of their own births! We need a new vocabulary. Anyway, I'm sticking with love child. I like it. And *this* '60s love child (like the majority of us) became an adoptee.

I was conceived in the summer of 1964. My birth mother was born in 1946 and had just graduated high school. She was a hippie of sorts, who sang folk music and played acoustic guitar. My biological father was born in 1941, served in the National Guard, and seemed to have modeled himself after the character Oliver in the movie *Love Story*, complete with preppie attire, tennis racquet, and little red convertible. Neither of my birth parents was married at the time, nor did they later marry one another. The two of them had next to nothing in common except for a fateful, hot, summer night . . . and nine months later, me. He never knew of her pregnancy (or me) and had already passed away by the time I found his family via DNA testing and genetic genealogy.

I was born and adopted in 1965. That year, 142,000 other love children were born who also became adoptees. For perspective, approximately thirty-eight of every 1,000 live births in the United States were love children in 1965. In 1970, the number rose to a record high of 175,000. Historically, and for perspective, 50,000 love children were born in 1944, 72,000 in 1950, and 93,000 in 1955. From there, the numbers climb steadily by 5,000 to 7,000 births per year, reaching the record high in 1970. Some blame the rising numbers on Elvis (his music and influence, of course)! The Supreme Court decided Roe v. Wade on January 22, 1973, giving women the right to abortion, and even so, the annual number of adoptions in the United States in the mid-1970s had not changed significantly compared to the annual number of adoptions in the mid-1960s.

Of course, for my adoptive family and me, the 1960s were a little less cool. My father was a pediatrician who kept Saturday hours and made house calls. My mother worked as an elementary school teacher. Almost nine years into their marriage and after a series of miscarriages, they adopted me and purchased their first home. My mom left her teaching career and became a housewife, which was common for the times. Today, we call housewives "stay-at-home moms" because of the overwhelming number of mothers who work full time outside the home.

Fifteen months later, in 1966, my brother Gordon was born to our parents. For Gordon and me, the 1960s were the time of cloth diapers and bottles, playpens and preschool, tricycles, boo-boos, our first family dog, coloring books and crayons, cartoons, our family's first color television, blocks, bubble baths, and bedtime stories. Good times and precious memories.

OUT OF THE MOUTHS OF BABES

I have a small handful of vivid memories from my early childhood. On November 5, 1968, my mom took me with her to vote in the presidential election. Richard M. Nixon would become president. It was midday, and we waited in line outside a school for what seemed like an eternity. Of course, when you have not yet entered preschool, waiting in line at the supermarket for five minutes can seem like an eternity.

Finally, it was our turn! My mom took me by the hand into a voting booth. I had never seen one before. It was a tall, dark-green metal contraption that had a curtain rod and curtain attached, with lots of little levers and a big handle coated with shiny red plastic. My mom pulled the handle all the way to the left and *swoosh!* The curtain closed, and she scooped me up into her arms. She instructed me on the purpose of the levers and pointed with her left hand to the levers she wanted me to push. She taught me that as citizens, we have a voice called a vote and that our voice matters.

When all the chosen levers were pushed, I placed my right hand on top of hers, and together we moved the handle back to the right and *swoosh!* The curtain opened. That was the day I learned to vote.

My dad usually arrived home from work around 6:00 p.m. As soon as I heard the garage door open, I ran downstairs to greet him. As he stepped into the house, I shouted, "Daddy! Guess what? I voted today!" I was so proud of myself and wanted him to be proud of me, too—after all, I had just learned that voting was a big deal.

"Wow! You did?" he asked. (Of course, he already knew that my mom had planned to take me with her).

"Yes! And you know what?"

He looked at me curiously.

"*My voice* matters!"

My parents got a chuckle out of that one, but I was beaming. I was three-and-a-half years old.

I believe that this experience instilled in me, at a tender age, the belief that I can and should use my voice to create the changes I'd like to see in the world. It's no wonder that I'm passionate and vocal about reforming discriminatory adoption laws. Thanks, Mom!

THE CHOSEN CHILD

In the summer of 1969, shortly after Apollo 11's lunar module *Eagle* landed on the moon, my mom told me a story called "The Chosen Child" for the first time. My brother and I were in our parents' bedroom watching cartoons before breakfast (a Saturday morning ritual in our home) and my mom told me the story during a commercial.

The story goes something like this: Once upon a time,

Mommy and Daddy fell in love and got married. One day we decided we wanted to start a family, so we went to the hospital and looked through the window of the baby nursery. You were the *prettiest* (or insert another positive word here—the *handsomest, most wonderful*, etc.) baby in the nursery, and we knew right away that you were the baby who was meant for us. So, when you were three days old, we brought you home and called you Geraldine (or insert child's name). You are our *chosen* child.

I remember considering whether or not she was telling me the truth and feeling certain that she was. I also remember thinking that it didn't matter because she was and always would be my mom, and I was and always would be her daughter and . . . I was hungry. This entire thought process took mere seconds.

Afterward, she asked, "Do you have any questions?"

And I said, "Yes. Can we have French toast for breakfast?"

As an adult, I asked my mom about this story, and she conveyed that I was also the *loudest* baby in the nursery. "In the late 1960s, child psychologists published books advising adoptive parents on how to tell children they were adopted," she said.

She explained that it was suggested that parents tell their child a story called *The Chosen Baby,* by Valentina P. Wasson, when they were preschool age and repeat it until the child understood that he or she was adopted and not *naturally* born to their parents.

By the time I was in the first grade in 1971, I understood that my brother came from "Mommy's tummy" and I did not. I came from a hospital nursery. I remember thinking, "That explains a lot," in terms of why I didn't look like either of my parents, yet my brother did. I was different. I was their "chosen

34

child," according to my mom's version of Wasson's story that she told me. Even so, I didn't feel any more or less special to them or any more or less their child.

In the second grade in 1972, I went to a friend's home after school for a playdate. We went up to her room to play, and she showed me an illustrated book, authored by Margaret Sheffield, called *Where Do Babies Come From?* Flipping through the pages together made me realize that being my parents' chosen child no longer meant that I came from a hospital nursery— it meant that's where my parents must have found me after I came out of *someone else's* tummy. There was never any discussion about *whose* tummy and, until my teen years, I didn't ask. I believed that they must have known this and either didn't know who that woman was or there was some other reason they chose not to tell me.

ARE YOU MY MOTHER?

That same year, there was a book sale at our elementary school. I remember perusing the tables covered with books, and I went home with a wonderful book called, *Are You My Mother?* by P. D. Eastman, published in 1960. In the book, a mother bird is sitting on her egg, which is about to hatch. She flies off to look for food, anticipating that her baby will be hungry and hoping the baby will stay put. The baby bird (a truth seeker!) hatches from his shell, and his mother isn't there, so he sets off to look for her. He approaches a kitten, a hen, a dog, and a cow and each time asks, "Are you my mother?" Of course, none of them is his mother. He continues searching, asking the question of a boat, a plane, and a large yellow power shovel, which drops the baby bird back into his nest. Then mother returns and asks the chick if he knows who she is, and he says, "You are my mother."

I loved that baby bird! He knew what it was like to be me! Ever since I discovered that I came from *someone else's tummy*, I looked at all women, wondering if they were the mother whose tummy I came from. I wondered what that woman looked like and if I'd recognize her if I saw her. I wondered where she was, why she left me in the hospital nursery, if she were looking for me, and if she would one day return. I never discussed this with my parents, and they seemed not to notice that my search for my birth mother had begun.

Is it any wonder that years later, I'd find myself on the telephone asking women whose names matched the one my birth mother used on my adoption papers, "Are you my mother?"

When I was a child of elementary-school age, we would sometimes bump into acquaintances of my mother in the supermarket or the beauty salon whom I had never met before. I frequently heard (and endured) the questions they whispered—in the kind of whisper than can be heard from three feet away. "Is she the adopted one?"

I remember thinking how obnoxious they were. I was standing right there, and everyone in line or nearby could hear them. Sometimes, they'd gush, "Oh, Doris, she's beautiful," as if I were a possession versus a person. I often noticed, by the way their eyes darted back and forth between the two of us, when her acquaintances were struggling to see a resemblance between us and failing. One did not need to be a rocket scientist to figure out that I was adopted. My mom had platinum-blond hair, blue eyes, and fair skin, and I have dark-brown hair, dark-brown eyes, and I am more olive complected.

In the absence of a reply from my mom, some would

36

continue, "She must look like her father." Sometimes my mom would just change the subject, and other times she'd affirm their comments by saying, "Her father has dark hair and dark eyes." This was a point of confusion for me, especially after having been told "The Chosen Child" story a few times and being made to feel special, in my own right, for being *chosen* by my parents.

Children are often smarter than their parents give them credit for. Even at the tender age of six, they know that hushed comments or omissions mean there is something to be ashamed of or that what is being said is somehow unacceptable to speak of in normal tones.

I realize that in those moments, my mom was protecting me from feeling different from my brother. However, what I learned from those experiences was that it was okay for people who are close to us to know the truth, but it was "nobody else's business." The defensiveness of the last comment (my mom's words) taught me that being adopted was something to be hidden or ashamed of, for some reason. So much for the era of social revolution!

MY CAREER AS THE FAMILY GENEALOGIST

In the summer of 1975, our family moved from the town of Greenburgh, New York, to Scarsdale, New York; both towns are in Westchester County, about twenty-five miles north of midtown Manhattan. My career as the family genealogist inadvertently began with a fifth-grade homework assignment. Each student was tasked with interviewing a family member who had emigrated to the United States and document that person's journey. I wondered what any of us would do if we *didn't* have such a family member, but I did. Our mother's mother, whom my brother and I called "Nana," was born in Poland in 1907. She used to tell us about her trip to Ellis Island on a very large ship, the *Finland*, in 1913. She was six years old and remembered it vividly.

My dad had a tape recorder—the kind that weighed a few pounds, took several large batteries, and came with an AC adapter and a handheld microphone with a little stand and an on/off switch. I inserted a blank cassette tape, pressed "play" and "record" simultaneously, and interviewed Nana as she spoke of her trip to Ellis Island from Poland, with her mother (whom our family called "Little Bubbie") and younger siblings.

I think the only thing I said into the microphone was, "Nana, tell me about your trip to Ellis Island," and she filled the tape, talking for almost an hour. I was amazed and could see the movie of her experience in my mind's eye. She was a little girl when she opened the front door of their small flat in Poland and saw Cossacks riding down the cobblestone street on horseback, capes flying and swords on their belts. The Jews were being persecuted. Nana's family were orthodox Jews who spoke Yiddish and kept kosher. She would never forget the fear on her mother's face when she grabbed Nana by the forearm, pulled her inside, and locked the door.

She remembered the mountain of baked goods her mother made for their journey to America and that they were confiscated on the ship and never returned as promised. They didn't speak English. She told of her uncle and one of her siblings taking ill on the boat. She went on and on. I knew how fortunate our family was to be able to record Nana's journey as she remembered it, not just for ourselves but for future generations, as these were the kinds of stories that our ancestors often took to their graves.

Long before the age of ten, I understood that Nana was not

my biological grandmother, but that didn't matter . . . she may as well have been. She was my nana from the time I was three days old. There were no car seats in 1965, and it was Nana who held me in her arms in the back seat on the way home from the hospital.

I remember thinking that her story was my story because we were family, and this was how part of our family came to America. Nana was one of the people who taught me how to love and how to think . . . how to grow, learn, laugh, laugh at myself, and evolve . . . how to grieve, endure, forgive, and how to thrive. She loved to laugh and loved children. She fanned the flame of my spirited nature and appreciated it, whereas my mom tried relentlessly to tame it. Nana is very much a part of who I am.

FANNING THE FLAME

Our friendship (Nana's and mine) began when I was in nursery school. I got in trouble for refusing to participate in nap time. I was never much of a napper, and I wanted to stay at my easel to finish my finger-painting masterpiece. I was wrist-deep in red and orange paint. The teacher called from across the room, telling me to go back to my desk and put my head down. "I don't want to. I'm not tired," I said and continued painting. She walked over to my easel, towering over me, and repeated herself with a raised voice, so I ran—around the room. You'd have run, too. She was scary! She chased me, and around and around we went.

While I was running, I called her a "big, mean, bully" and told her I was going to tell my parents on her "for yelling at me and trying to *force me* to take a nap." Some other preschoolers got up from their desks to join in the rebellion. (*Circus* was more like it). When it was time to go home, I had a long nasty note from the teacher stapled to my lovely blue coat. It was raining, so we students stood outside at the top of the stairs with our teachers, waiting for our parents to pull up under the porte-cochère. When my mom pulled up, I noticed my brother in the back seat, and Nana got out to escort me to the car. She glanced at the note, shot the teacher a dirty look, ripped it off my coat, stuffed it into her purse, and off the four of us went to lunch at 14 Karats, the restaurant we frequented at B. Altman's department store.

Many years later, I found that easel painting folded in half in a scrapbook of things from my childhood that my mom kept for me. I still have it, and it always reminds me of that day— the day I learned that it's okay to challenge authority (especially when it is unreasonable or nonsensical) and march to the beat of my own drum. The first time my parents ever heard the story was when I eulogized Nana at her funeral in 2004, four months before her ninety-eighth birthday.

Thanks to Nana, my fifth-grade homework assignment never ended. For years, Nana shared family tree information with me. She told me about her parents, her aunts and uncles, their spouses and children (her cousins), her siblings and *their* spouses and children. She told me who was named for whom, where everyone lived, and where everyone was buried. I would write it all down, amazed that she knew so many of their birthdays, anniversaries, and death dates by heart. Family was everything to her.

Sometimes when we went to her apartment in Brooklyn, New York, she would take out her old photo albums and share stories about people who were no longer with us. I found it fascinating to see the faces of the relatives whose names I had written on the family tree—it brought their stories to life for me. I also marveled at the family resemblances, as I had never looked like anyone in my family . . . or anyone I ever knew, for that matter. Anyway, this is how I first learned that the way we keep our loved ones alive is by talking about them and sharing their stories.

As an adult, I loved spending time with Nana. Sometimes I'd pick her up and take her for her weekly hairdo, followed by lunch at Epstein's, our favorite deli, in Hartsdale, New York. We often ribbed each other and joked. She was a little under five feet tall but could finish a lean, corned beef on rye, half a side of fries, and two cups of hot tea with lemon in only *two* hours. I used to tease her about that, saying, "Take your time, Nana. The dinner crowd won't be here for *another* two hours!"

And she'd say, "Geraldine, I'll give you a *zets!*" and we'd laugh. Zets or *zetz* is Yiddish verb that means "to hit," but she would gesture with two fingers and a poking motion directed toward my ribs. When I close my eyes and think of her, I can see her face, her smiling eyes, and can almost smell her Chanel No. 5. When she was finished eating, she'd ask, "Are you ready to go?" which always struck me as funny, since I had been ready to go for at least an hour. But it didn't bother me. I loved her and her company, and I knew that being there, eating her favorite sandwich, made her happy. I loved making her happy. We would make an afternoon of it, and after lunch, I would take her to the town beach in Rye. We loved it there. We would find an unoccupied bench on the boardwalk to sit on, look out at the water and talk about whatever came up, and she'd say things like, "You do what you can do, and it's all you can do." There was a simplicity to her wisdom, and in all my time knowing her, she was never wrong. How I miss her.

I once asked Nana how she most wanted to be remembered, and she said, "For helping people." Me too. She will always be precious to me—more precious than rubies.

TWEEN AND TEEN YEARS

Mindi and I met in the fifth grade and have been best friends ever since. We both loved music, took piano lessons, and sang in the school chorus. After school and on weekends, we used to sing into our hairbrushes to her older siblings' records, such as Sergio Mendes's *Brazil 66* album, and to the records of some of our own favorites, like the Captain and Tennille. We'd make up dance steps and spend hours refining our routines.

Our interest in dance music began with the movie and soundtrack to *Saturday Night Fever* and was nurtured on the 1978 Bar/Bat Mitzvah circuit. Almost every second or third weekend for a year, many of us got dolled up, watched friends read from the Torah at Westchester Reform Temple, and danced at the parties that followed. Our friends' parents rented swanky catering halls, country club ballrooms, and private dance clubs. Some rented tents and hired bands or DJs to play at their homes. Within an hour, all the girls' shoes were usually in a pile somewhere . . . as they would later be at our weddings.

I often wondered where *my* musical genes came from. Mindi's mother taught piano and was a composer in her own right; and her maternal grandfather, Giuseppe Ferraro, was a pianist, music professor, and an ASCAP composer. I am musical, as Mindi is, and both of us composed for piano, but no one in my family was particularly musical.

It was around this time that the thought occurred to me that we likely inherit much more than our physical traits. Almost thirty years later, I would discover that my birth mother was a singer, songwriter, and musician in her youth, and her paternal great-grandfather Max ran his own music school. Her paternal grandfather Louis played second trumpet in the New York Philharmonic for forty years and was known for being able to play by ear in any key. (So *that's* where I get it from!) Louis's brother George played clarinet in the orchestra, and his sister Fannie was a piano teacher. You just can't make this stuff up.

MAGICAL MYSTERY TOUR

In the eighth grade, I became interested in astrology. Mindi and I would read our horoscopes in the teen magazines and local newspapers, and sometimes we would ride our bikes to the supermarket and buy the little astrological scrolls on colored paper that came in plastic tubes. Each zodiac sign had its own color, description, and horoscope inside. We loved them!

Before homeroom at Scarsdale Junior High School, we would meet at the pay phones by the gym, insert fifty cents, and call the Jeane Dixon Forecast. Her recorded messages would begin with an announcement of the date, and then she'd launch right into, "Hello, Taurus," or whatever your sign was, and you would hear your daily horoscope. We were hooked, and it was fun to see if Jeane was right or full of beans. This interest later led to fun with fortune tellers, Ouija boards, and other mystical things. We were on our own Magical Mystery Tour, eleven years after "the British Invasion." More musical, magical, and mystical stuff later.

"YOU DON'T *LOOK* JEWISH..."

Around this time, I also grew increasingly curious about my true heritage and ancestry. I had another dear friend, Nancy, who lived across the street. Nancy was adventurous and athletic. We were going to be astronauts! (That didn't last long). We hoofed it to Crossway field for our softball games, baked brownies, listened to Elton John tunes on the jukebox in her basement, and played tennis in my driveway. We always seemed to be *doing* something.

Nancy and I spent more time at her house than at mine. Her mom was more laid back and permissive than my mom. Okay, *everyone's* mom was more laid back and permissive than mine! This is not just my own opinion or experience—but if you didn't know us then, you're just going to have to take my word for it. The more controlling my mother attempted to be, the more rebellious I became. I even bought a leather jacket in high school just to irritate her, even though I was a varsity runner for all four years and ran out of room for stripes on my letter-jacket sleeve.

Anyway, in the mid- to late-1970s, Nancy's mom often remarked that she thought I looked like Ali McGraw, the actress. I didn't know who she was at the time, but I wondered what she looked like and if my birth mother looked like her.

Nancy herself was (and still is) a genuinely good soul and fellow animal lover without a mean bone in her body, and she would often unabashedly say exactly what she was thinking. She was the first person to tell me, "You don't *look* Jewish."

What could I say? The thought had often occurred to me, too. She was right. I was raised in a Jewish home and in the Jewish faith, but I didn't "look Jewish." Her remark fueled my desire to know whom I looked like and to have answers to the questions I had been asking for most of my life.

That day after school, I asked my mom if she knew anything about my birth mother. She said the attorney had told them that she was "a Jewish high school student," so I spent most of my life believing that was true and assumed that my biological father had to be "something else," since I "didn't look Jewish."

I asked my mom if she knew what my birth mother looked like and if I resembled her. I was about thirteen or fourteen the first time she told me about the day she and my dad brought me home from the hospital. We were standing in the kitchen, and my mom was preparing dinner.

"It was daylight saving time, and the social worker who was supposed to meet us at the hospital got her wires crossed and wasn't there," Mom said. "The attorney called and told us that I would have to be the one to take you from your birth mother instead, but that she was to *think* that I was the social worker. He said that your birth mother and your grandmother would be holding you and standing outside on the hospital steps, because adoptions were not allowed to take place within hospital walls. I was told that they would hand you to me and I wasn't to say a word. I was to take you from them, get in the car, and drive away. Your grandmother was tall and thin with snow-white hair, and she had a bob cut. Your birth mother was wearing a kerchief. Her head was down, her face was red, and she had been crying. I really couldn't see her face. She handed you to me, and I walked with you to the car. Your father was driving, and I handed you to Nana, in the back seat, and we all went home."

I replied, "Wow, I'm *so sorry*, Mom." I remember thinking what a sad story that was, and I felt heavy hearted. I can only imagine what it must have been like for my mom to literally take me from the arms of my sobbing birth mother, with her mother (my biological maternal grandmother) standing beside her.

My adoption was a private adoption, arranged by an attorney six months into my birth mother's pregnancy, so my parents didn't know if they would be adopting a son or a daughter. My mom had hoped, prayed, and waited almost nine years to become a mother and had to go through *that* the day they brought me home. "My God," I thought. It must have been difficult or even impossible to feel joyous. The day her dream came true was the day my birth mother went home without me and my mom had to witness her grieving. I remember thinking that I didn't know if I'd be able go through what either one of them did that day.

My mom told me the story a few times over the years, and each time it was exactly the same. She never mentioned how she felt, and I didn't ask her. I already knew. I heard it in her voice.

In junior high school and high school, friends would sometimes innocently ask, "What are you?" referring to my "nationalities" (now called "ethnicities" by the DNA-testing companies.) I would tell them that I was adopted, that my birth mother was Jewish, and that I didn't know anything more about her or my biological father. Sometimes these conversations were how I found out that *other* classmates were adopted. Scarsdale was a small town, and by high school, most of us adoptees were aware of each other. There weren't many of us. Years later, I helped some of them identify their birth parents.

I found it interesting to hear the people who knew me speculate that I might be Italian, Greek, Scots Irish, German, Russian, the list goes on . . . but only some of that resonated with me.

Mindi's mom, Juliette, whom I and all of our close friends affectionately called "Mom," used to say, "Ger, come on! We all know you must be Italian. Of course, you are Italian!" That always made me laugh because she had no idea, and yet she was totally serious and declared it as if it were a known fact. She wouldn't entertain any other possibilities.

As it turns out, I have ancestry from *all* those places and more, but I wouldn't learn the half of it until reuniting with my birth mother in 2007. I wouldn't learn the other half until 2017, when I identified my biological father via DNA testing and genetic genealogy. He was, in fact, half Italian. This would have come as no surprise to Juliette!

CH-CH-CH-CH CHANGES

My teen years were strained between my mom and me. This is not to say there weren't good times—there were many. Two ladies, one younger, one older, in the same house, with different ideas of how their lives should be lived, is a recipe for . . . well . . . let's just call it *tension*. This wasn't unique to my mom and me. I knew others (boys and girls alike) who experienced similar issues with their parents at that age—namely orders, pushback, disapproval, and the ensuing arguments. Maybe that's why we all loved David Bowie's song "Changes" so much. We could relate.

The tension lessened when I went off to college and dropped off even more afterward. I guess we all mellow with age, though I'm certain the word *mellow* has never been used to describe either of us. For perspective, it is important to add that I loved my mom and always will.

I CARRY YOUR HEART

My mom passed away in 2004, after a four-year battle with metastatic breast cancer, and only two months after Nana passed. If I had never known what and who was truly important in life before, I knew it after lying in bed beside her for almost a month at Calvary, the hospice in Bronx, New York, spooning to prevent her from rolling onto her back, which was painful for her. I became acutely aware—to a level where there are no words. At the end of the day, it's all about who you love and who loves you; it's about the people who have become a part of us, shaping who we become. That's it.

Our family was devastated by her loss (and Nana's), and our lives were forever changed. At some point in my grief process, my suffering eased with the epiphany that Mom had never really left us—she never can. She will always be with us—in our hearts—as a part of who we are. There was comfort, peace, and truth in this for me, and I don't mind revealing myself like this, if doing so will ease even one person's suffering and loss.

This book is really all about easing loss for adoptees and others with unknown parentage—the loss of parts of self, of relatives, and of heritage—and about healing by discovering the truth of who they are. My goal is to create awareness for their plight (our plight) and share my strategy for making living in the know a reality for them.

FOR MY MOM

> *Here is the deepest secret nobody knows*
> *(here is the root of the root and the bud of the bud*
> *and the sky of the sky of a tree called life; which grows*
> *higher than soul can hope or mind can hide)*
> *and this is the wonder that's keeping the stars apart*
> *i carry your heart (i carry it in my heart).*
>
> —*E. E. Cummings*

This verse from the famous love poem "[i carry your heart with me (I carry it in]" exquisitely expresses the depth of feeling we have for our loved ones, whether a partner, family member, or friend. They become a part of us that we carry with us in life and beyond their passing. They live on in us.

I carry my mom with me. She is with me all the time, even when I'm not paying attention. Whenever I'm about to leave a room, I still hear her voice saying, "Geraldine, turn off the lights. We don't support Con-Edison." I smile and turn back to flip the switch. I miss you, Mom.

SISTER FRIENDS

By high school, Mindi and our close friend Christine had each lost a parent. The losses they carried and shared were devastating, to say the least. We knew each other's parents, we were like family, and I shared in their losses.

Not knowing who my birth parents were was a different kind of sorrow. I was the girl who fell out of the sky into a hospital nursery and was not "naturally" anyone's, while virtually all who surrounded me were "naturally" someone's and resembled one another. Parts of me were *missing* . . . my blood relatives, my heritage . . . and the chances were good that they were gone forever and that my heritage would forever remain unknown to me.

Each of us was intimately aware of the others' pain—the source and the holes those losses created in our hearts. Then and for years to come, we had deep discussions about the way our losses affected us—our anger, our sadness, our powerlessness, and our fears—revealing dimensions of ourselves to one another that few others knew about. We were more like sisters than friends. I thank heaven for these amazing women and for my other "sisters" whose names do not appear here. I am grateful for our history and for their presence in my life. They are my *ohana,* my family.

HANAI OHANA

Years later, a friend who knew that I was adopted said, "You are my *hanai* ohana." She learned the term in Hawaii and said it's Hawaiian for "the family that you choose." I encourage you to research this term and its use in the Hawaiian culture.

Ohana means "family," whether or not related by blood. Friends are often called ohana. *Hanai* means "adopted or one's adopted family members," and the word is usually reserved for explaining the circumstances to someone who is unaware. Hanai ohana. What a lovely sounding term—more lyrical than "adopted," though the meaning is the same.

Due to the small and close-knit nature of the communities on the Hawaiian islands, Hawaiians traditionally regarded everyone as part of an extended family. Families were large and many of them were also genetically related. Over time, and as communities grew exponentially, this idea morphed into the cultural phenomenon of all inhabitants (native and newcomers) regarding one another as ohana, similar to the way many of us feel today about our friends and former classmates from our hometowns and college towns.

In Hawaii, adoption is completely different than it is on the mainland. And though it is hard to imagine the Hawaiian model working on the mainland, it's interesting to note the differences.

Adoption in Hawaii is often informal. Family members adopt the children of other family members or neighbors and raise them as their own. The adoptee, for the duration of his life, has two mothers, though the father situation varies. Both love the child, and the child is raised knowing both of his mothers, though the adoptive mother is the central presence in the child's life.

They are all ohana. The child is free to be loved by both of his mothers. The concept that the heart expands and that there is enough love to go around for all members of the adoption triad—the birth parents, the adoptee, and the adoptive parents—is depicted beautifully in the award-winning 2016 movie, *Lion*. If you haven't seen it, I highly recommend it.

THE LATE '70s AND EARLY '80s

In the summer of 1979, before my freshman year in high school, I met my first love, Matt, at the Scarsdale Municipal Pool. He was almost four years my senior, had just graduated high school, and was to attend American University that September. I sometimes shared with him how I felt about not knowing the truth of my origins. He knew that my mom and I had a strained relationship, and many years later, he told me, "Even I was afraid of her."

That made me laugh. Matt was a warm, well-liked, personable, and athletic young man from a good family. He was always polite and respectful of my mother. Even so, she kept the exchange of pleasantries brief, she appeared unmoved by his efforts to ingratiate himself, and she made sure we both knew my curfew. My mom was a no-nonsense parent, whose hierarchical communication style and demeanor was well known to my friends. Unlike some of their parents, my mom was not one to spend time truly getting to know her children's friends or making them feel like extended family when they came to visit. That said, she did so with a select number of my friends in my early adulthood and beyond.

In high school (the early '80s), by day and during the week, I was a preppie (jeans, T-shirts, and crewneck sweaters, and clogs, penny loafers, or docksiders with no socks—you know the type). I was a varsity cross-country and track and field athlete (two-mile relay and open 800-meter) and a rock 'n' roller. Sometimes in the late afternoon, Mindi and I would meet at Christine's house and bounce around to the B52s and other new-wave music in Chris's living room. We would have sleepovers on weekends and stay up late, watching *Saturday Night Live* and talking about *everything*, the way best friends do.

On Saturday nights, my friends and I led somewhat secret lives. We would occasionally get decked out and disappear into Studio 54 and other popular dance clubs in New York City, Port Chester, and New Rochelle, thanks to older friends, free passes, and our fake IDs. Those were the days when Michael Jackson's "Billy Jean" and Earth Wind and Fire's "Let's Groove" were rocking the world and long lines formed outside the New York City clubs, where the bouncers decided who was allowed in and when. We would tell our parents that were studying together—We were! We were learning how to moonwalk!—and would sleep at one of the others' homes.

We'd sing and dance all night, mostly just with each other, and leave the clubs, dripping with sweat, for a 2:30 or 3:00 a.m. breakfast at the Eastchester Diner. If our parents ever discovered what we were doing and where, we would have been grounded . . . for life.

On summer weekends, Mindi and our friend Peter and I would go to Jones Beach on Long Island (West End II, for the best waves), Pete, whom we'd known since ninth grade, was a few years older and drove a cute little Ford Mustang with a cassette player. He would drive, and Mindi and I would pack lunch and beverages for the three of us. On the way there and back, we sang along to our favorite tunes. (Mindi and Pete dated on and off throughout high school and college. They now have been married for thirty years and have two beautiful daughters—my "nieces," who have called me Aunt Gerri since they were little.)

Our day trips to the beach were a favorite summer activity that became an annual tradition, and sometimes other friends joined us. During those years, I made the acquaintance of a few fellow high school students who were adoptees, some of whom have remained my good friends over the years. I don't remember exactly how the topic of being adopted came up, but I do remember that some of us knew this about the others before we actually met.

Scarsdale was a small town, and the high school had about 1,600 students. While not everyone knew each other well, it was not uncommon to tell a friend that you were adopted and then hear from that friend who else she knew at school who was adopted or had an adopted sibling.

I remember some of the conversations I had with the other adoptees. We compared notes on when we first learned we were adopted and how we felt about it. All of us had been adopted shortly after birth, and all of us were told about our adoptions when we were preschool age. Some had a sibling who was also adopted and others, like me, had one sibling (or more) who were born to their adoptive parents, either before or after them. All of us called our parents *Mom* and *Dad* and didn't think of them any differently than our nonadopted siblings and friends thought of their parents, nor did any of us feel we were treated or parented differently than our sibling(s) were.

All of us wondered about our birth parents' nationalities, as we called ethnicity then—English, Irish, Italian, Scandinavian, etc.—and none of us liked having to respond, "I don't know," when asked by friends and acquaintances, "What are you?"

A common sentiment was that it didn't seem fair to us that nonadopted people knew their true ethnicities and we didn't . . . nor would we ever be allowed to know. We all knew our adoption records were legally under permanent seal, though our parents had shared with us whatever they'd been told about our birth parents, which was mostly just that our birth mothers were young, unmarried women. We knew we'd likely never know anything else about our birth parents, and most of the time we didn't think about it. But when it did come up, it was an uncomfortable reminder of how we were different from the vast majority of people we knew.

From the teen years forward, each of us recognized and personally felt the injustice that people in vital records offices and surrogate courts (where our adoptions were finalized) had access to our birth information, our original identities, and those of our birth parents, while that information would be withheld from us for life. We were all victims of the restrictive New York state adoption laws of that day. And we all knew there would be no way around them, even after we reached the age of legal majority.

4

Coming of Age

My search for my birth mother began in earnest on my eighteenth birthday. My mom and dad had always been aware of my need and desire to know about my own ethnicities and my birth parents, particularly my birth mother, and were (*thankfully*) unthreatened, understanding, and supportive of my need to live in the know.

I was glad that I could be open with them. My parents knew (and I made the point of telling them) that I wasn't interested in searching because I wanted to replace them. After all, they had been my parents all my life and no one could ever change that or the love between us. Still, I had to find my birth mother; it was my quest. She held the key . . . to me.

I knew that my mom kept my adoption papers in her safety deposit box at the bank. I once asked to see them, curious about my birth mother's name, and my mom said I could have them on my eighteenth birthday and not before. If you knew my mom, you would understand there was no sense whatsoever in asking a second time.

SAY WHAT YOU NEED TO SAY

The day arrived. It was my eighteenth birthday. In the weeks prior, I had given a lot of thought to how I would raise the topic. I didn't want to hurt my mom. But I would have to ask her eventually, because I couldn't let it go. I knew she'd honor her word . . . but asking her worried me. I needed to wait until the right moment . . . or something. I had no idea how I was going to ask her. I was late getting downstairs for breakfast, and when I walked into the kitchen, I was unusually quiet. I avoided eye contact with her.

She knew something was up and said, "What's the matter?"

"Nothing . . . why?" I said as I stared into the refrigerator with my back to her. I was stalling for time more than anything else. I was still in search of the *right* words.

She said, "Nothing? Come on . . . out with it." We never really minced words. We said what we meant and meant what we said, come what may. We were always *real* with each other.

Suddenly, I was on the spot. I had that "now or never" feeling you get in your stomach on the high dive, just before stomping on the edge of the board with both feet and diving head-first into the water, wondering if you'll have enough air in your lungs to make it back up to the surface, because sometimes it's a close call and anyone's guess.

I decided to go for it. I had *no idea* what was about to come out of my mouth. There was no time to find the right words and no way of knowing how it would go. I took a deep breath, turned to face her, and asked, "Now that I'm eighteen . . . do you . . . think I can see my adoption papers?" I was glad to have been able to summon the courage and relieved that what came out didn't sound *that bad*. I am reminded of this moment whenever I hear John Mayer's song, "Say," as it expresses how

I was feeling at the time, what I chose to do—and the way I live my life.

Without skipping a beat, she said, "I don't know; can you?" She always corrected my grammar. (I thank her for it now.) And part of her personality and sense of humor was that she was a chop-buster extraordinaire.

"May I?" I asked again, properly.

It was a Thursday, and she explained that the bank was in Ardsley, near my dad's office, and that we could go together on Saturday morning. I was cool with that . . . a few days' delay in exchange for *that* conversation being over. Good deal! I felt myself starting to breathe again.

I downed a tall glass of orange juice, threw a yogurt and an orange into a brown-paper lunch bag, and kissed her good-bye. "Thanks, Mom. See you later."

She said, "Not if I see you first," her standard reply.

I got into my car and headed to school, thinking on the ride in that the conversation had gone *a lot* better than I thought it would. Though Mom could be stoic, she seemed fine with it, which was a great relief. I didn't give it another thought until Saturday.

Saturday came, and we hopped in the car and took a ride to Ardsley. By the time we pulled into the bank parking lot, I was filled with nervous excitement. What would I discover about my birth mother . . . and about myself?

We entered the bank, and my mom requested access to her safety deposit box. I followed her into a small, carpeted room with a built-in desk, a chair, and a white shutter door with a brass knob. Moments later, the teller appeared in the doorway with the metal box. Mom took it and shut the door. She placed the box on the desk, lifted the lid, and took out my adoption papers, which had been folded to fit a standard-sized mailing envelope. My eyes were fixed on the papers, and without a word, she handed them to me. I didn't look up to see her face. I was afraid of what emotions I might see in her eyes, and I was overwhelmed by my own.

I unfolded the papers. Most were legal-sized court documents. I wondered what memories seeing them again held for Mom. They looked so *official* and smelled like old library books. On them, I saw my birth mother's name, her mother's name, my adoptive parents' names, and the attorney's name. For the first time, I was able to *have* and *view* the facts concerning the beginning of my life. Then, for the first time, I saw my birth name: Female Rubenstein.

I asked my mom if she knew where my birth mother was from, and she said, "The attorney told us that she was a Jewish high school student from northern Westchester."

At last, I knew my birth mother's name—Carol Rubenstein. According to the relinquishment of parental rights document, she had been a minor. In 1965, the legal majority age was twenty-one, so I now knew that she was under twenty-one when I was born, and she likely was born between 1944 and 1948. Her mother's name and signature appeared on the same document. My maternal grandmother's name was Gail Rubenstein. Lastly, Mom had told me they were from northern Westchester County, New York. I thought, "Well, how hard can *that* be?" I was sure I'd be able to find her and that it wouldn't take long with all the information I had.

On the way home, I had an epiphany. I realized that my mom had insisted on waiting until my eighteenth birthday for *my* sake. She wanted to be sure that I had the emotional maturity to handle the papers, my birth mother's and grandmother's names, and my own feelings. Looking back, I'm glad I made the choice to let her know that I'd had that realization.

MYSTICS AT THE MALL

Having gotten our start as pop singers in front of the huge mirror in her parents' finished basement, by high school, Mindi and I were music freaks. We loved music! We knew almost every word to every song on the radio and sang in the car (in two-part harmony) almost everywhere we went.

Like most teenage girls in the area, we were no strangers to the Galleria shopping mall in White Plains, New York. It's still there. One day, Mindi and I went there on a mission to Sam Goody's for some new records (yes, the twelve-inch vinyl kind) by the Police and U2. We found what we were looking for and then we drifted into Waldenbooks, located on the same floor. While perusing the books and magazines, I noticed a box labeled Mythic Tarot. I was intrigued. I opened the box and said, "Hey Min. Check this out! Tarot cards!" Of course, we left with them.

I fell in love with my Mythic Tarot deck, and it came with a book. I read my own cards and read cards for my friends and wrapped the deck in a special silk scarf when it was not in use. I still have it, though I haven't used it in many years. I've come to realize that the answers to life's greatest questions are most often found *within*—and that has never been truer than it is today, with DNA testing, a topic we will cover in Part 4.

THE STUFF YOU LEARN IN COLLEGE

I went to New England College, in Henniker, New Hampshire, a small, liberal arts college located in "the only Henniker on earth," a place that will always be close to my heart. (If you blink while driving through the blinking light in the center of town, you will miss Henniker.)

When I attended in the mid-1980s, the entire student population numbered about six hundred. The college itself was built into the town, and we attended the majority of our classes in white clapboard houses subdivided into classrooms. The average class size was twenty students (and some had as few as twelve) and we were on a first-name basis with our professors. A few miles down the road was Pats Peak, a ski area. There were also apple orchards on the mountain, which everyone referred to as "the Peak."

New England College was a very special place, and the student body grew together like one, big, extended family, which in some ways is easier to recognize now than it was then. Many of us have managed to stay in touch all these years and did even before the advent of social media. I kept busy with my classes, was a DJ at the college radio station (WNEC-FM), sang in a rock band, met my college sweetheart (the bass player), and made a handful of close friends who would become lifelong friends.

My college "besties," with whom I've remained in touch all these years, are Beth and Kelly. Both of them were (and still are) deep thinkers, philosophers, and both knew about my search for my birth mother.

Beth was practical and grounded and a beautiful person, inside and out. She was wise for her years, and her wisdom was based in logic. She also had a cheeky sense of humor, and you knew she loved you if she busted your chops. None of this has changed! We used to take road trips to Vermont, where her family had a summer home facing Lake Champlain. Sometimes her mom and dad were there, and Mom (I called her "Mom" too) would make spaghetti and meatballs, salad and garlic bread. When we walked in, the house smelled like heaven. How we missed home cooking!

Beth and I were confidants, and she knew all about my search, as did Kelly. When my birth mother and I were reunited, Beth drove three hours to Henniker and met us at Daniel's restaurant for lunch. In many ways, my search had become Beth's search during those years, and it seemed fitting to ask her to join us for a portion of our reunion. Watching one of my best friends talking with my birth mother about our search for her was heartwarming and unforgettable.

As it turned out, my birth mother was living just four miles outside of Henniker in 2007. She and her husband had moved to Weare, New Hampshire, just four miles down Route 114S from Pats Peak, about ten years after I graduated from NEC. One of the first photos that my birth mother emailed to me after our first phone conversation was of her and her sister, my aunt Solene, standing on a covered bridge.

I call her back immediately upon receiving it and asked, "Is that the covered bridge in Henniker?"

She replied, "How on earth would you know that? There's only one Henniker on earth, and it's a tiny town."

I replied, "Because I went to New England College, and I walked over that bridge for four years."

You *really* can't make this stuff up!

Kelly, like me, was attracted to mystical things. He was a fellow truth seeker, and we did a lot of spiritual growing up together during our college years. We believed we were kindred spirits, and about twenty years later, we discovered that we are distant cousins, connected by the Howland/Tilley (*Mayflower*) and Partridge families. In addition, we share common Scottish highlander ancestry as descendants of Robert the Bruce, King of Scots in the 1300s. Amazingly, we are cousins several times over, though we didn't know it then.

We'd stay up for hours sharing the stories of our lives

and debating concepts like free-will choice versus destiny, sometimes with wine involved. We'd hike the cross-country ski trails in Henniker and get together in the summer months, having discovered that we'd grown up only ten miles apart. (He lived in Greenwich, Connecticut). I got to know and love his family. His mother, Anne, is also my distant cousin.

For a time, during our college years, Beth and Kelly and I were like the Three Musketeers. Periodically in those days, I had a recurring dream about being reunited with my birth mother. I would dream that I was on her doorstep (in my dream, she lived alone in a light-gray Victorian with a front porch) and rang the doorbell. She invited me in, and I noticed that I resembled her greatly (which later turned out to be so). She directed me to take a seat on the couch and then left the room. When she returned, she was carrying a brown-paper shopping bag filled with birthday cards tied up with ribbons, and she told me there was a card for each year we'd been apart since my birth. The dream was so vivid, I remember waking one morning saying to myself that I have to be sure to call her later. Instantly, I realized that our reunion was just a dream.

It felt like a cruel fate, not being able to know who and where she was. It made me wonder if I were repaying some karmic debt or being punished somehow.

One night in late fall, Kelly came over after dinner. The town was so small that most all of us lived within walking distance and often dropped in on one another. Few students had landlines, and this era predated cell phones and the internet. It was dark outside and raining. I told him about my recurrent dream and how the last time it had seemed *so real*. Neither of us were sure what it meant, and I wanted answers. I needed answers. We decided to consult the Mythic Tarot.

I went to get my cards, and when I returned to the living

room, Kelly was sitting on the floor. This was not our first time consulting the cards together. I closed my eyes, shuffled the deck, and asked, "Why can't I find my birth mother?"

I spread the cards out facedown and pulled one from the deck. Kelly looked the card up in the book. I asked, "What does it mean?"

"Hold on. I'm looking for it," he said, thumbing through the pages. I watched him, waiting to hear. "Here it is," he said.

I have long forgotten which card it was, but I will never forget its message. Kelly read it aloud: "When it no longer serves you not to know, you will know."

"What does *that* mean? How does *not knowing* serve me?" I asked.

"Try again," he said. "And this time, ask for clarification."

I shuffled again, asking the same question and for clarification of the first message. I spread all the cards out again, facedown, and took my time choosing another card, hoping that this time, I'd choose the *right* card.

The deck has seventy-eight cards, all with identical black backs. I chose the very same card. "Hmm! Oh well," I said. "It looks like I'm not going to get an answer tonight." We moved on to other inquiries.

But there is an old saying that the Universe throws pebbles, then it throws stones, then it throws pianos. (I added the pianos—the original word may have been *bricks*.) The meaning is that we keep getting the same message over and over again, until we *get it*. Sometimes the Universe throws a *gem* (a fateful message), though we may not recognize it as such at the time. I had just gotten pinged twice with a gem via that tarot card, but it took me more than thirty years to realize it.

THE SEARCH FOR CAROL RUBENSTEIN

The details of my search for my birth mother and the truth of my origins could fill a book. I may one day write that memoir—but this is not it.

One would think that with the information I was given, my search would have been relatively simple. I was wrong. It was impossible.

It would take twenty-four years and my birth mother's voluntary contact with ALMA for us to be reunited. I would discover that the names that she and my maternal grandmother used on my adoption papers were aliases. Most young mothers were not of legal majority age, and as such, at least one of their parents was required to sign the legal relinquishment of all parental rights.

I visited many libraries, spending untold hours in the New York Public Library's Genealogy Room perusing stacks of birth indexes. I went to the state and county records rooms, in Albany and Westchester, respectively. Over the course of two years, I systematically visited every high school in Westchester County to view yearbooks in search of Carol Rubenstein.

I took notes, made photocopies, perused microfilm, and made countless calls to Rubenstein families in search of a Carol whose mother was Gail. My little spiral notebook quickly grew to a three-ring binder, which eventually grew into a small filing cabinet.

In the early 1990s, home computers were relatively new, and I had purchased a list of the addresses of every Rubenstein family nationwide from a website. There were 2,250. With the help of a dear friend, Diane LeVierge, a birth mom I'd met at a local meeting, we mailed each Rubenstein family a handwritten letter over the course of a year. Back then, it was widely accepted that photocopied letters might be thrown out, whereas handwritten letters received attention and replies. We received a 10 percent response rate, and no one knew my Carol or Gail. I never could have done that alone. Diane and I are still in touch, and I'll always be grateful for her love, friendship, and encouragement to persevere against all odds.

I attended local search and support group meetings hosted by ALMA, Concerned United Birthparents (CUB), and Adoption Crossroads members in their homes. I read everything available on the topic of *adoption search*. I ran personal ads in the local newspapers. I hung out mostly with the birth moms, thinking that if my birth mother were actively searching for me, I'd find her among them—not among the adoptees, though I attended those meetings too.

I learned a lot of the ins and outs of adoption search (the old-fashioned way) and read books on the topic. The majority of my mentors were birth moms who had surrendered their children for adoption between 1954 and 1970. It had occurred to each of them that my birth mother must have used an alias, as no one could crack my case. Some of these women, such as my dear friend Sandy Musser, who dedicated her last book to me, were pioneers in the Adoption Reform Movement. They were in their forties and fifties when I was in my early twenties, and they are still active in the adoption community—some as vibrant and ballsy as ever! I will always cherish their leadership in the fight for adoptee equality, their solidarity as women and members of the adoption triad, and the friendship I found (and still share) with these remarkable adoptee-rights activists.

Yes! Adoptee-rights activists. While it is not common knowledge, some birth mothers were pioneers of the Adoption Reform Movement and fought side-by-side with adult adoptees for adoptees' right to obtain their original birth information when they reach the age of legal majority. Many birth mothers deeply resented that the fact that they'd had virtually no choice in surrendering their children for adoption, and years later, did whatever they could to ensure that when their children came of age, they would easily be able to find her if they chose to search.

A common thread that runs through many adoption-search cases is that birth moms deliberately left clues in their child's birth name . . . like a breadcrumb trail through the forest. For example, if the child were a boy, the birth mom might use the biological father's first name and her own maiden surname.

The majority of states that still restrict or prevent access to adult adoptees' original birth information hide behind what they call *birth mother privacy* claiming that it's the state's responsibility to protect birth mothers' privacy and anonymity, when in fact, the state statutes that established adoption procedures never provided for confidentiality with respect to public inspection or for secrecy between the parties involved.

What this means it that birth mothers were never promised or guaranteed privacy or anonymity, nor did they insist on it. This is not to say that some didn't want privacy then or later; it was simply not part of the law.

The sealing of adoptees' original birth information was actually intended to protect the new identity of the child and the privacy of his/her adoptive parents, as there was concern that young mothers might go looking for their surrendered children, thereby disrupting the lives of the adoptive family—particularly in cases where the adoptive parents hadn't told the child that he or she was adopted. So, in fact, these procedures were put in place to protect the anonymity and privacy of the adoptive family *not the birth mother*. More on this topic in chapter 7.

My own search inadvertently became the school in which I learned to help other adoptees as a *search angel*, a volunteer in the adoption community who helps others complete their searches. I was a search angel for over fifteen years, but I was unable to complete my own search. During those years, there were false positives when I identified people whom I thought *must be* my birth mother, only to discover they were not. There was great, joyful anticipation followed by deep disappointment. It was an exhausting emotional rollercoaster, and I had to hop off from time to time in the name of self-preservation.

I had registered with ALMA in 1991, after seeing a reunion made possible by ALMA between a birth mother and her daughter on the *Oprah Winfrey Show*.

In the years after we 1960s and 1970s love children came of age, ALMA's registry became filled with adoptees and birth mothers in search of their parents or children. Matches were made based on date of birth, birth location, and other factors on the registration form. My birth mother had written to ALMA in 1996, but I had recently moved from Connecticut to New Jersey and had neglected to update my address with ALMA. My search had been so difficult for so many years that I stopped believing that finding her could be that simple.

In 2003, I moved to Georgia with my now-former husband, John, to be closer to my brother and his family. At that time, my mom, Doris, was undergoing treatment for breast cancer, and my parents' hope and plan was to relocate to Georgia too. While I had mixed feelings about leaving the area while my mother was sick, my parents encouraged us and said they would eventually be there to join us. Sadly, my mom's dream of watching her only grandchildren, Bryan and Meredith, grow up was never realized. My dad moved to Georgia after her passing.

HARRY'S MARKET

Within a week of my forty-second birthday in 2007, I was shopping at the local farmer's market (Harry's) when I noticed a woman pushing her little girl in a shopping cart. The woman had platinum-blond hair and a fair complexion, and her daughter had olive skin and long, dark hair. Seeing them reminded me of my mom and me at the supermarket when I was a little girl.

I walked on and noticed an employee handing out food samples. He greeted me and handed me a small white cup filled with what looked like chocolate-covered raisins. My favorite! I popped one in my mouth and took a bite and . . . yuck! It was a chocolate-covered coffee bean, and I felt like I had a mouth full of coffee grounds. My mom loved coffee candies, coffee ice cream, coffee everything, and I never did. I found a napkin and walked on.

Ah! Thankfully, or so I thought, there were little white cups on a tray up ahead. The store was promoting its own brand of juice. I grabbed a cup to rinse my mouth and . . . yuck! Grapefruit juice! I love the smell of grapefruit but can't take the bitterness. But guess who loved grapefruit? The moment that occurred to me, I got the chills. "Okay, Mom, I get it now. You're here. You must be dropping in for my birthday. I hope you and Nana are okay. We all miss you so much. Listen, I'm going to be forty-two in a few days, and God is busy. Please bring me my birth mother for my birthday. I'm out of hope and have exhausted all options. I really need my search to be over. Thanks. I love you." And then I let it go, finished shopping, and went home.

A few days later, John and I were getting ready to have our home-office painted, which required moving a large, wooden filing cabinet out of the room. Even empty, it would weigh a ton. I began to empty my drawers and came across my ALMA folder. In light of my mom's visit at Harry's market, I thought, maybe I should contact them. Later that evening, I sent Marie Anderson an email asking her to update my file with my new address.

COMING OUT OF THE DARK

The next day, April 18, 2007, the phone rang. It was Marie. We exchanged greetings, and then she said, "Are you sitting down? You have a match!" I almost dropped the phone.

I understood what she'd said, but I didn't believe it. She read aloud the letter that my birth mother had sent in 1996. Immediately, I thought of my mom. Tears streamed down my face. "I don't believe it," I said to myself. "Thank you, Mom."

Because I was already an experienced intermediary in adoption search, I asked Marie if it was okay if I called her myself. She gave me her number, and I called, but the number was disconnected. I called Marie back, and she worked her magic. Within fifteen minutes, she gave me a working number. (I never ask *how* she does this; I'm just glad to know she can!)

I called and got an answering machine. I left a message and tried to be patient. (Let's just call patience a "developmental opportunity" for a Taurus like me.) I called again at 3:00 p.m. A woman answered and said she had just come through the door with groceries. I told her who I was, where I was calling from, and that I had just been in touch with ALMA and heard the letter she sent in 1996.

She said, "You found me, baby! That's me!"

We talked for almost three hours, during which time she

remarked on the date and asked me if I knew what that day was.

"No." I said.

She told me that April 18 is the anniversary of the midnight ride of Paul Revere. She recited the famous poem from memory. I paced while we spoke, and my whole body tingled the way a foot does when it falls asleep. The "juice" was running through me, and my greatest fear was that I was going to wake up and discover it had all been a dream. While she talked, I found myself doing things to make sure I wasn't dreaming, such as looking myself in the mirror and gently slapping my cheek.

I learned that my birth mom had indeed used an alias (as did her mother) on my adoption papers. She was not Jewish, though her paternal grandfather was. She also told me that I have six half siblings, all of whom had known about me since they were old enough to talk. We exchanged pictures via email while we talked and decided, after a three-hour marathon, to take a dinner break. Afterward, we spoke for another few hours, sharing abbreviated stories of our lives. Later that same evening, we both expressed the desire to meet in person, as soon as possible.

Three days later, on my forty-second birthday, it felt as if the big dipper had poured love all over my life. I received an email from each of my half siblings (whom I affectionately refer to as "my sibs," which also includes their spouses). They all said they'd always known about me and hoped I'd find them one day. They included pictures of themselves and shared excerpts from the stories of their lives.

My aunt Mene (the wife of my birth mom's brother, Val) called me, and then each of my siblings called. That day, I spent over eighteen hours on the phone. My left ear was hot, my neck hurt, and my heart was full. My prayers had been answered.

When the answer comes from above it's *unmistakable.* You don't just get what you've asked for . . . you get infinitely more, and it just keeps coming. The love and joy I heard in their voices and in my own was a dream come true.

My birth mom and I decided to meet for the first time on Mother's Day weekend in 2007, at her home in New Hampshire. We met at the airport in Manchester. I expected to see her at the luggage carousel, but she wasn't there. I learned that there was another set of carousels on the other side of the airport, so I decided to walk there. She must have had the same inclination, because suddenly, we spotted one another in the breezeway that connected the two areas. We were the only two people there.

There were no words. We dropped our bags and hugged, rocking from side to side for several minutes. In those minutes, I felt the hole in my heart begin to close. The emotion I was feeling was *relief*—as though someone had finally removed the thorn that had plagued me, on and off, for most of my life. Suddenly, it just *didn't hurt* anymore. I could feel my soul exhale. My search for her was over. She was alive. She wanted to meet me. She loved me. My prayers had been answered. This is what most adoptees who are searching hope and pray for.

That weekend, I met my birth mom's husband and my grandmother, who lived with them. We spent the days talking and perusing old family photos. We pulled an all-nighter one night; the way girlfriends do. We drank wine, and I laid my head on her lap as she read to me from Rudyard Kipling's *Just So Stories*, a book she used to read to my half siblings when they were children. She told me she had written a song for me during her pregnancy, and she sang it to me while playing the guitar. The likenesses between us were astonishing. I was a watered-down version of her. She was expert in much of what I had found myself attracted to or interested in throughout my life.

The next morning, as I was getting ready to hop in the shower, she knocked on the guest room door. She had a gift for me. It was *Mayflower*, a book by Nathaniel Philbrick. I thanked her and opened it to read the inscription, but there was none.

"You forgot to inscribe it," I said.

"Go get in the shower," she said.

When I got back to the room, the book was on the bed, and on the title page, she'd written:

Once upon a time, oh, Best Beloved, some of us fled persecution—ventured out and came to be and multiply, on these then-foreign shores. Among these precious few that survived and faced the world and all its hardships, you have been descended.

As of this book's publication, there are approximately 35 million *Mayflower* descendants, of which you are one that will forever shine in my being and heart. We were born with inner maps and with them we have at last found each other.

Love always, Mom

She opened with "Once upon a time, oh, Best Beloved" as Kipling does in his stories as a remembrance of the night before. I could not keep from crying when I read her inscription, and to this day, I get choked up whenever I read it aloud.

One night, after her husband went to sleep, we decided to hop into the large hot tub on her back deck. It was a clear night, and the sky was filled with stars. The New Hampshire sky can be so clear and pollution-free that it's sometimes difficult to find the constellations among all the visible stars. Ahhhh! Hot water, crisp air, and a starry sky on the weekend my dream came true.

We looked up at the stars, and I said, "Look, there's the big dipper."

"Yes, and there's Cassiopeia, Pegasus, and the Seven Sisters," she said. "We should go upstairs and do your chart, dear."

All I could do was giggle. You just *can't* make this stuff up. Of course, I told her all about my interest in astrology, natal charts, and the tarot cards.

Mother's Day came, and we went out to dinner in neighboring Henniker, at the Colby Hill Inn. After dinner, we returned to the house, and my grandmother was sitting on the couch with a very somber look on her face. I asked her what was wrong. My birth mom had already told me that she was trepidatious about my visit.

My grandmother felt guilt, shame, and fear. She knew, as we all did, that she was the one responsible for our separation. She was ashamed to have to face me all these years later as an adult, and she feared that I was angry with her. Also, I was in the prime of my life, and she was in her nineties and felt vulnerable.

"I'm just an old lady, living in the middle of nowhere, in a little apartment over the garage, and all this karma is finding me," she said.

I was actually tickled that she used the word *karma*.

I told her that my parents had always said that my birth mom was too young to raise me and that adoption was the choice most families made then, under those circumstances. I told her that she had made the right decision, and I had a great life. I told her that I was never angry with her or my birth mother. "It's okay, Grandma," I said, and I could see her begin to breathe again.

She told me that when I was born, she was working as a school teacher, had four teenagers and an unemployed husband, and that keeping me was just not possible.

"It's okay, Grandma. We're together now," I said, and she cracked a small smile. Lord only knows what was going through her mind or what it was like for her to see me and know me as an adult. I'm glad that she and I had the opportunity for that closure. We knew each other four and a half years before she passed away in 2011.

My birth mom and I attended her burial in Mendham, New Jersey, behind the Hilltop Church, at the feet of our ancestors, her fifth great-grandparents, Ebenezer and Hannah Hayward Byram. Ebenezer Byram established The Black Horse Inn (in 1742), the Hilltop Church (in 1745) and named the town Mendham, on March 29, 1749.

My birth mom and I spent the rest of our reunion sharing the stories of our lives and confiding in one another about it all . . . the good and the bad. We didn't hold back or put on airs (neither of us is that kind of person) or try to paint rosy pictures for one another. We just told it like it was, and that felt great. It gave each of us real insight into the other and her life experiences.

I waited to ask my birth mom who my biological father was. I was interested in getting to know her and had so many questions about her and her family that there would be plenty of time to talk about him later. But I did ask. It took another ten years to identify and locate my biological father.

A little over a year later, my six half siblings and I were together for the first time at our brother Ib's wedding to Lisa in California. They rented a large beach house, and after the ceremony, I drifted into the kitchen to grab a drink. Ib was already in there doing the same. "What does it feel like being *you* today?" he asked. I tried to speak, got choked up, started to cry, and we hugged. He said, "It feels like there has never been a time when you weren't with us. You *just fit* perfectly." He had described exactly how I was feeling. There was a familiarity and affection on a soul level. We had no conscious memory of one another, but we *knew* each other. I can't describe it any other way and have often heard my adoptees describe their experiences similarly. It's amazing. A moment later, our sister Ro drifted in and wrapped her arms around both of us. Then, in came our other siblings and their spouses, and we were in a group hug that must have looked like a huddle from the living room. That is a day I will never forget and one that forever changed my life for the better.

At that time, I was in a failing marriage with a man who could not understand or could not care less about what was happening for me, nor did he want to join me at that wedding— but then, he seldom wanted to be a part of *any* family occasion. My birth mom, who spent almost a week with us, predicted aloud to me and my sibs that my marriage "will never last." She saw what I couldn't yet see—the end and all the reasons. I was still in denial and hopeful that things would work out, though I felt more alone and lonelier in that house with him than I felt when I was actually alone.

One day, I was talking about this with my half brother Hass, and he said, "Cut yourself loose and let it all sink to the bottom. It's never going to change, and it's only going to get worse. The *worst* thing you can do is have kids with this guy. You want to have a happy life, don't you? You have to love *yourself* enough to leave the situation and create the space for the right person to come in. It's a leap of faith you have to be willing to take, if you really want to be happy." Hass is a man of few words, but when he says something, be prepared to hear it straight up and to be blown away. Meeting my sibs and their spouses in person, seeing how they all were with me and with each other, being a part of that experience, and remembering other significant others I'd had who would have *wanted* to be by my side at a family celebration underscored all the reasons I had to leave him. It strengthened me to do so. We were divorced within the year, and I never looked back.

As it turned out, Hass was right. Had I not taken that leap of faith, my life would be very different today. Gloria Estefan's "Coming Out of the Dark," best describes what I went through, prior to my divorce, and the happiness I have felt since, knowing it was the right decision for me.

A PLATE FULL OF ANCESTORS

In the years that followed our reunion, my birth mom and I would travel the world (on the phone, using Google Earth) visiting the home countries of all the ancestors we discovered together. We knew all the family lines, via the male line of descent, but we didn't know who all our great-grandmothers and their families were. So, we researched them and visited their places of origin online. "Where do you want to go tonight?" she'd say.

"I don't know," I'd respond. "How about Budapest or Gothenburg?"

Some of our ancestral family lines are documented back to the 1300s in the book, *Burke's Peerage*, a well-known genealogical resource. I entered each of their names into our family tree and suddenly had what my birth mother called "a full plate of ancestors," too many to count.

What began as an exercise of playing "fill in the blanks" morphed into a journey of self-discovery. As I learned more about my ancestors, I came to realize which of those family lines echoed more so than others in me. I was no longer the "chosen child" who fell out of the sky into a hospital nursery. I had *lineage*. Some of my ancestors were American pioneers, minsters, prolific writers, merchant traders, musicians, and farmers/planters. Others sat on the thrones of Europe during the Middle Ages. It's *all* in there.

NATURE OR NURTURE?

People who are not adopted often ask me, "Which of your mothers do you think you are more like?" It seems they're looking to solve the age-old question of nature vs. nurture, or they may be interested what percentage of me matches each mother—50 percent? Or 80 percent? I tell them that their question can be likened to "What's your favorite color?" The answer depends on what we are talking about—flowers, cars, carpeting? So, for the record, my answer is: it just depends on what we're talking about.

After my birth mom and I were reunited (three years after my mom Doris's passing) she and I developed a close, adult mother/daughter relationship. She taught me how to crochet and how to make scallops in French lemon-cream sauce, homemade eclairs, and the best oatmeal cookies I've ever tasted—with pine nuts and golden raisins. We both love to cook. She shared everything she knew about her heritage with me, and we did a lot of myth-busting together, as documents and facts replaced fictitious family lore.

Each of my mothers has contributed, in her own way, to the person I have become. I could not be who I am without both of them. Some of my tastes, interests, talents, personality traits and inclinations come from my birth mother, and some come from my adoptive mother. The way I see the world and operate within it and my values (those I was raised with) come from my adoptive mother and father. So, I am like all of them, in addition to a whole bunch of other stuff that I inherited elsewhere and picked up from my friends and their families. The joy (what tickles me) is knowing where it all comes from, and that it *does* come from somewhere—really, a whole bunch of *someones*, lest we forget that we are all a little bit of everyone we have come to know well, blood relation or not.

Also, there's a school of thought that we are all no more than fifty-second cousins to one another. This is likely true, as genetically, we're all 99.9 percent identical. That's a fact. It's only about one-tenth of 1 percent of our DNA mutations that make us all look and behave so differently.

TEN YEARS POST-REUNION

In the ten years after my reunion with my birth mother, I was still unable to identify and locate my biological father. During that time, I periodically found myself asking the question, "Why can't I find him?" Each time I asked, I remembered that fateful tarot card I pulled in college and thought, "When it no longer serves you not to know, you will know."

I was still in need of the reason . . . or thought I was. I left the cards in the drawer and tried to accept the original message.

Those words became a mantra for me. The more I found myself repeating them, the more I found peace in them and tried to let go and trust in the Universe. The promise of finding him *someday* was there, but it would not be on *my* timetable.

Inevitably, the question of who and where he was gnawed at me. It's great to trust in the Universe, but I'm also a big believer in employing the *law of action.*

In 2013, six years post-reunion with my birth mother, I was talking on the phone with our cousin Jack, who had just taken a Y-DNA test to further research his father's lineage. He was aware of my predicament and suggested that I take an autosomal DNA test. I asked, "What's that?" And the rest, as they say, is history.

When my DNA results came in, I tried to interpret them on my own. I did see that I was 21 percent Italian, plus trace regions, so I knew that my biological father had to be half Italian, as my birth mom has no Italian ancestry. I had a few relatively close DNA matches/relatives (second and third cousins) but they were all on my birth mom's side.

Eventually, I reached out to two well-known experts, shared the details of my search and DNA results, and was told, "It's impossible. You're just going to have to wait for a closer match."

That was when—and why—I decided to become an expert in genetic genealogy. I wanted to find my biological father and the other half of the truth of my origins. It wasn't a career ambition; it was a *soul mission.*

Even so, and much to my dismay, I would later discover that those experts were right; without a closer match, it simply was not possible. The only difference was that by then, I fully understood all the details and nuances of *why* it wasn't possible. This was no consolation after metaphorically banging my head against the wall for so many months. Despite this roadblock, I persevered. I kept reading books, volunteering on others' DNA adoption search cases, and telephonically forming relationships with my distant Italian DNA relatives.

MI CUGINAS

Mi cuginas! My female Italian DNA matches/relatives. What an amazing group of women! These ladies became my genealogy partners in crime, trying to help me discover my paternal family line. We all live far from one another, in different parts of the country, and affectionately call one another *cugina,* which is Italian for a female *cousin.*

Our ancestors lived for hundreds (likely thousands) of years in the Palermo region of Sicily, though each of us knows but a handful of Italian words and phrases. Sometimes my cousins and I remark on how our ancestors are probably smiling on us, pleased that we have connected with one another and are connecting branches of the family that lost touch with one another over a century ago. It's a nice thought.

My cuginas and I are from an *endogamous population* (where for centuries, cousins married cousins). As such, we're likely not fourth to sixth cousins, but more like seventh to tenth cousins several times over. We may never be able to pinpoint our common ancestors, who we believe to be just two or three generations beyond our *brick wall,* where our research dead-ends in the absence of vital records that are not available online and may not be available at all. Our assumptions are based on the appearance in the early 1700s of common surnames in our trees. We know they existed and that we are family.

It took DNA testing, an ongoing education in genetic genealogy, and a few years of solving many other cases before I was finally able to identify my own biological father. All of my DNA matches (aka genetic relatives) were far too distant—fourth to eighth cousins—but at last I received a close enough DNA match to solve my own case. I call her "my DNA Angel."

To my surprise, my father's surname did not appear in the family trees of any of my DNA matches. Many of their ancestors were Palazzolos and Randazzos (and allied families) from Terrasini Favarotta, just around the bend from Termini Imerese, where, I would discover, my biological father's paternal side hailed from. (His mother's side was from Kaniska Iva, Croatia.)

OFF THE HOOK

My cugina, BetteJo in Mesa, Arizona, has access to all my DNA accounts. We met via Ancestry.com and have been close phone friends for years. She was the first person on my biological father's side who I spoke with after receiving my AncestryDNA test results. I had written to her brother (a fourth- to sixth-cousin match of mine) and BetteJo replied, as she manages his account. For years, while I was busy solving others' cases, BetteJo was popping into my accounts to see if a closer paternal DNA match had appeared among my DNA matches/relatives, in hopes of helping me put an end to the search for my biological father. After a few years, I seldom checked the accounts.

One summer evening in 2017, I was on a phone call with an adoptee, when BetteJo tried phoning me. I could see her call waiting, but it was not a good time for me to answer. When I didn't pick up, she called my cell phone number, then she called my home phone again, then my cell again. She was ringing both phones off the hook. That wasn't like her. I wondered what was up. I immediately called her when I got off the phone and asked, "What's up? Is everything okay?"

"You just got a really close match!" she said.

This was the match I had been waiting for. Within hours, I solved my case. I'm forever grateful to BetteJo. We share the gene for tenacity, though we're still trying to figure out exactly how, on each of our paternal Italian sides. I'm a DNA match to BetteJo's father, brother, sister, and nephew, though she and I share no DNA in common. I joke with her sometimes, asking, "Has your family told you you're adopted yet?" We later discovered that we are also tenth cousins once removed via our maternal lines, and direct descendants of Deacon William Crocker and his wife, Alice, who were among the early settlers of Plymouth Colony.

Genetic recombination is the explanation for our having no DNA in common, and it's common for cousins of this distance not to share any identical segments of DNA. For fun, we'd go online to GEDmatch.com together, (GEDmatch is an online service that compares members' autosomal DNA files from various DNA-testing companies) and BetteJo would lower the shared DNA threshold to 1 centimorgan, trying to find our shared DNA segment(s). We'd laugh, as GEDmatch suggests that relatives use 7 centimorgans as a minimum threshold, agreeing that 1 centimorgan is genetic dust—and we don't even have *that* in common.

I learned that my biological father had passed four years before I made contact with his family. He was one of seven siblings: a sister and six brothers. Close paternal cousins of mine helped me narrow my search to the man they believed was my biological father and suggested that I reach out to his daughter to see if she would be willing to take a DNA test. She was kind enough to agree, and her DNA test results conclusively proved my biological father's identity and the fact that she is my half sister.

Christmas of 2018 was a very special holiday for my Mangione relatives and me. More than ten of us gathered at my home, and it was a memorable occasion for all of us.

On a prior visit, my uncle Lou and his wife, Dawn, came for a long weekend, bringing about three hundred Mangione family photos from his childhood, which I digitized and shared with other branches of the family. Among the photos was my biological father's high school yearbook photo. We look very much alike. During our visit, Uncle Lou and I discovered things we share in common, including our love of food, wine, cooking together, and breaking bread with family. He is also a big hugger, as I am. "It's been ten minutes . . . get over here," he would say. Since then, his niece (and my first cousin) Koren and her husband have been to visit a few times. So much fun! I feel very fortunate to have found my Mangione family.

Believe it or not, another Mangione first cousin resided less than two miles from me when I lived in Georgia. We spent a lot of time together and developed a close friendship. She is the person who told me where our paternal grandparents are buried—a third of a mile from my former home in Danbury, Connecticut. What are the chances of that? You seriously *can't* make this stuff up.

FEELS SO GOOD

When I tell people that I discovered my natural father was a Mangione with Sicilian roots, they ask, "Any relation to Chuck?"

I don't know . . . it's a small island, and there is a chance we're distantly related. My ancestors were from Termini Imerese and emigrated to New York City, and musician Chuck Mangione's ancestors were from Agrigento and emigrated to

Rochester, New York. If we are cousins, we're more distant than third cousins, as I was only able to build his tree backward a few generations with information I found online.

If you know Chuck, please encourage him to take an AncestryDNA test, as most of my Mangione DNA relatives are in this DNA pool. Better yet, ask him to call me! I'd love to meet him, and I still love his (1977) hit song, "Feels So Good."

After discovering who my biological father was, I visited Aunt Mene, who surprised me by playing that song (she had the CD) in celebration of the end of my search. Living in the know **feels so good!**

WHEN IT NO LONGER SERVES YOU NOT TO KNOW, YOU WILL KNOW

My ten-year search for my biological father became the school within which I learned to help others with unknown parentage via genetic genealogy, much the way my twenty-four-year search for my birth mother taught me how to help other adoptees as a search angel using more traditional—now dated and less successful—methods.

I supplemented my knowledge base via traditional education that included textbooks, course work, case studies, and a master's-level genealogical research certificate program. Continued education is key in the field of genetic genealogy, as advancements are being made all the time, and professionals in the field must stay current. The learning curve is a deterrent for many, and it's likely the reason for the high dropout rate in classes.

As it turns out, the ten-year delay in finding my birth father was the Universe's way of sending me back to school. Had I found my biological father when I wanted to, I never would have become a genetic genealogist and author. Further, hundreds of adoptees might still be searching for biological family members and the truth of their origins, and this book would not be in your hands.

Everyone and everything in my path to date has led me here to you, and I am grateful for it all. I never could have imagined that the Universe had more in mind for me, or that during the course of my own searches, it would reveal my higher purpose to me, or that I would meet so many people who have become dear to me. This is how I believe the difficulty of my searches has *served* me and many others whose mysteries I have solved.

Further, the blessing of discovering the truth of my origins and the experience of getting to know, love, and be loved by members of my birth families has been profoundly healing after a lifetime of not knowing.

As a result, I have a deeper understanding of *the whole of who I am* in a way that was not possible before. That understanding has led, in the years since, to the blessing of being able to recognize as my natural partner the man with whom I plan to share the rest of my life.

In hindsight, I have come to realize that without first knowing, loving, accepting, and appreciating *the whole of who I am* on a deep, soul level, it would not have been possible for the two of us to meet one another on that level or to resonate as we do.

It is my passion and privilege to help others to discover the truth of their origins and to unite and reunite families, and I am glad that my journey to living in the know has become a part of yours. Everyone's journey is different, and I wish for you all that you wish for yourself.

PART 3

Adoption in the United States

5

The Adoption Reform Movement

The following is an abbreviated history of the Adoption Reform Movement in America.

As of the writing of this book in 2020, forty-eight out of fifty states in the United States place adoptees' birth and adoption records under permanent seal. This includes their original birth certificates (OBCs), court records, adoption agency or attorney's documents, legal documents such as the Relinquishment of Parental Rights and the Petition to Adopt, hospital records, and all other records related to the birth and adoption. This practice began in 1917 in Minnesota, and most other states jumped on the "seal and forever withhold" bandwagon between the 1930s and 1960s. But not Alaska and Kansas, which have never withheld adoptees' original birth information.

In 1953, Jean Paton (1908–2002), a forty-two-year-old adoptee and former social worker, began collecting adoptees' stories, which eventually became her book, *The Adopted Break Silence*. In it, she gives adoptees a voice.

Paton fought relentlessly for adoptees' rights to their own birth information. She became known as the mother of the

Adoption Reform Movement—a grass-roots band of adoptees and birth mothers that began forming in the mid-1960s when some states were implementing sealed-records practices and took hold nationwide in the 1970s.

Paton was also instrumental in founding the American Adoption Congress (AAC) and Concerned United Birthparents (CUB).

Adoptees and birth parents, I encourage you to learn more about Jean Paton and the history of the Adoption Reform Movement. Check out the AAC and CUB. Look into ALMA (Adoptees' Liberation Movement Association) at www.Almasociety.org. ALMA is a mutual-consent, nonprofit reunion registry with an active nationwide network of volunteers and professionals. Also look into ISRR (the International Soundex Reunion Registry) at www.ISRR.org. ISRR is also a mutual-consent, nonprofit reunion registry. All of these groups formed in the early 1970s to support adoptees and birth parents and are still alive and kicking today.

Many adoptees and birth parents are unaware that support is available. All of these organizations will tell you that it will be a happy day in the adoption community when their services are no longer needed. Sadly, no one believes that day will ever come—not in our lifetime, anyway.

The movement has seen several waves, and over the years, "the fight for open records" morphed into "the fight for unrestricted access to our own original birth certificates." (*Open records* refers to all records pertaining to the adoptee's adoption, not just the original birth certificate).

Each state governs the filing, issuance, access, and storage of vital records for life events (i.e., birth, death, marriage, and divorce) that occur in that state. Legislative reform to *restore* the rights of American adult adoptees to access their own original birth certificates has been slow. I use the word *restore*, since prior to 1917, all adult adoptees possessed this right, the same as every other adult citizen. I use the word *slow*, as I was born in New York in 1965, and it wasn't until 2020, long after I had found my birth families, that I was legally able to access a copy of my own original birth certificate. Others were born and/or adopted in states where sealed-records statutes adopted a century ago still stand.

6

Who Is Affected?

According to the US Census Bureau, there were over 329.5 million people in the United States as of August 2019. Of the total population, it is estimated that approximately 78 percent (or 257 million people) are eighteen years of age and older and approximately 22 percent (or 72.5 million people) are under the age of eighteen.

Of course, it is understood that no government reporting agency can possibly account for *all* living people within its borders at any given time, let alone those who fall within a particular subgroup. However, these numbers and statistics give us a general idea of population demographics and provide a basis for comparison.

There are no hard statistics on the number of adoptees living in the United States today. The numbers vary based on the sources consulted. Why? One reason is that a nationwide reporting system for legal adoptions only existed during the Baby Scoop Era, when several government entities, including the United States Children's Bureau and the National Center for Social Statistics, collected information that was voluntarily supplied to them by the states. Another reason is that currently, the United States has no state or federal requirements to count children who are surrendered for adoption. The only adoption statistics that are reported by state governments involve the adoption of children in public foster care.

And, of course, there is no data on informal, black-market or otherwise illegal adoptions that circumvent the system and subsequent government reporting.

NUMBER OF ADOPTEES IN THE UNITED STATES

The number of adoptees in the United States can be estimated via a review of annual adoption statistics collected between 1945 and 1975. It is estimated and generally accepted that between 2 percent and 4 percent of the current United States population are adoptees and that 2.5 percent of all children under the age of eighteen are adoptees.

In order to arrive at an estimated number of adoptees in the United States, let's use an average of the accepted 2 percent to 4 percent range and agree that 3 percent of all people in the United States are adopted. That means 9.8 million people are adoptees.

For the same purpose, let's accept and agree that 2.5 percent of all children under the age of eighteen are adoptees; 2.5 percent of 72.5 million people is approximately 1.8 million adoptees under the age of eighteen.

Assuming that 9.8 million of all people in the United States are adoptees and that 1.8 million of them are under eighteen years of age, we can estimate that there are approximately 8.1 million adopted adults in the United States as of 2019.

While there is no way to know how many illegal adoptions circumvented the system between 1945 and 1975, we assume they were not the norm. As such, I'm going to assume they comprise 2 percent or less of total adoptions. It could be more or less.

I'm going to add that 2 percent (approximately 200,000 people) to our 9.8 million and arrive at a nice round number of ten million adoptees, *with the understanding* that this figure could be off by million or two in either direction. For perspective, in 2018, the total population of the state of Georgia was 10.6 million.

There are approximately ten million adoptees in the United States today. The Adoptee's Family Tree illustrates that approximately 260 million lives* are touched by adoption in the United States.

(See graphic on page 95.)

THE ADOPTEE'S FAMILY TREE

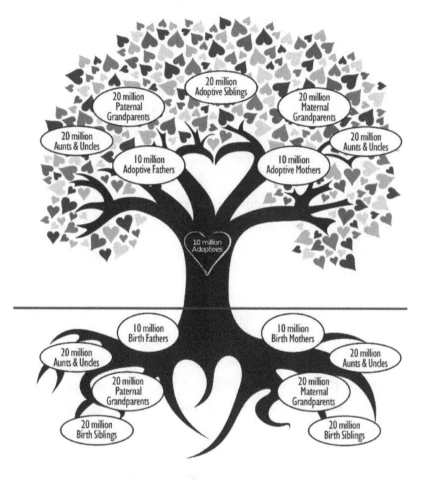

These are low estimates. Some families may have more or fewer siblings, aunts, and uncles. Cousins, spouses, descendants, and close friends of adoptees are not included in these estimates.

The estimates in the Adoptee's Family Tree do not include the millions of children who were placed in foster families or aged out of the foster system by reaching age eighteen without being adopted. As per Childwelfare.gov, in 2017, over 690,000 children were in foster care.

Further, those estimates do not include others with unknown parentage, such as those born in foreign countries (fathered by American soldiers)—or raised by their mothers or other biological family members, with no knowledge of their birth parent(s).

As per Lifescience.com, researchers believe that about 4 percent of men are unknowingly raising a child who is not genetically their own. The *paternal discrepancy rate*, as it is called, is believed to affect approximately one in twenty-five families in the United States.

If we conservatively estimate that an additional two million people were raised in foster families (and either were not adopted or aged out of the system) and that an additional 4 percent of the total population (thirteen million people) have an unknown biological father, due to paternal discrepancy, then an additional fifteen million people in the United States have unknown parentage.

Add ten million adoptees to the other fifteen million people with unknown parentage, and that yields a total of approximately **twenty-five million Americans** (or roughly 7.6 percent of the population) with unknown parentage, for whatever reason.

Since 22 percent of the total US population was under the age of eighteen in 2019, we can estimate that 22 percent of the twenty-five million adoptees and others with unknown parentage in the United States were under eighteen years of age in 2019. This translates to approximately 19.5 million adults and 5.5 million children in the United States with unknown parentage. (These are rough estimates that may vary by a few million in either direction.)

For perspective, the population of the state of New York was 19.5 million and the population of Texas was 27.5 million in 2019. Google the statistics for your state, as twenty-five million is an enormous number that is difficult to fathom otherwise.

We can safely assume that the percentage of adopted people can vary widely by state, based on the statistics available between 1945 and 1975.

My estimated nationwide average of those with unknown parentage is 7.6 percent. It appears that **between 5 percent and 10 percent of the total population** is a realistic estimate. But, of course, it would be ideal to know the actual numbers.

7

An American without a Heritage — The Plight of the American Adoptee

> *The idea of an American without a heritage is simply un-American. This is the plight of millions of American adoptees—and it should not be!*
>
> *—Geraldine Berger*

I was born in New York State, a state that until January 15, 2020, sealed and forever withheld the original birth certificates (OBCs) and by extension, the true identities of American adult adoptees. This was a travesty of justice that is still perpetuated in forty of the fifty states, and Washington, D.C. Thankfully, Governor Andrew Cuomo signed the Adoptee Rights Bill into law. Thank you, Governor! I hope leaders in the states that still withhold adoptees' birthrights will follow suit.

In many ways, mine is the story of millions of other American adult adoptees who continue to endure the plight of having been born and adopted in states whose governments withholds our OBCs, while the majority of American citizens (predominantly nonadopted persons) enjoy unrestricted access to their OBCs.

Nonadopted adult citizens may request their OBCs from their state's vital statistics office, pay a fee, and receive them. The vast majority of adopted adults who request their OBCs receive the following response: Access Denied.

No American citizen should endure discrimination by his or her own state government, whose sworn duty it is to protect and defend the rights and privileges of its citizens equally, merely because he or she was adopted as an infant. Unrestricted access to the OBC is the right of all other (nonadopted) adult American citizens—and it's our birthright, too.

How can the US government stand aside and allow states to pass laws that strip American citizens of their human, civil, and constitutional rights and falsify birth records? It's been happening to American adoptees since the 1930s and it should not, as this practice is in direct conflict with our values as a nation. It needs to stop.

The widely accepted account of when American adoptions became cloaked in secrecy goes something like this. Early in the twentieth century, starting with Minnesota in 1917, states began moving toward protecting the privacy of participants in the adoption process by closing court records to public inspection. Then, in the 1930s, 1940s, and early 1950s, virtually all states took the further step of imposing a regime of secrecy under which adopting parents and birth parents who were unknown to one another would remain unknown and adult adoptees could never learn the identity of their birth parents. While a few states closed original birth records to adult adoptees at approximately the same time they closed adoption records to the other parties, most states proceeded much more slowly with respect to adult adoptees' access to birth records. In fact, as late as 1960, some 40 percent of the states still had laws on the books recognizing the unrestricted right of adult adoptees to inspect their original birth certificates. It was only in the 1960s, 1970s, and 1980s that all but three of those states changed their laws to close birth records to adoptees. At the same time, a growing national advocacy movement, the Adoption Reform Movement, was pushing for greater openness in adoption by encouraging many states to establish passive and active registries through which adult adoptees and birth parents could attempt to seek information about and establish contact with one another.[2]

Alaska and Kansas are the only two states that have never sealed and withheld the OBCs of adoptees. The only states today (as of this book's publication) that provide adult adoptees with unrestricted access to their OBCs (no vetoes, redactions, restrictions, or "partial access" for some born between certain years and not others) are Alabama, Alaska, Colorado, Hawaii, Kansas, Maine, New Hampshire, New York, Oregon, and Rhode Island.

Sealing and withholding OBCs from adult adoptees is blatantly discriminatory and an egregious violation of our basic human rights, as well as our civil and constitutional rights as American citizens. This practice disgraces us as a nation, particularly because we pride ourselves on being the worldwide beacon of freedom, justice, equal rights, and democracy.

Our credibility is further compromised by the fact that out of 193 member states of the United Nations, we are one of only two states that has not ratified the United Nations Convention on the Rights of the Child (UNCRC). The remaining one, Somalia, is a Third World country. The UNCRC is the most widely and rapidly ratified human rights treaty in history. The

---

2—"The Idea of Adoption: An Inquiry into the History of Adult Adoptee Access to Birth Records," *Rutgers Law Review* 53, no. 367 (2001), http://www. americanadoptioncongress.org/pdf/idea_of_adoption.pdf.

United States signed the Convention, indicating its intention to ratify, but has not.

When correctly implemented, the UNCRC gives children the right to know and have access to their original families and the official record of who they are.

It's time to restore the rights of American adult adoptees and thus, restore the United States to the status of the true role model for other nations that we pride ourselves to be. We talk the talk, however our credibility as a nation ultimately rests on walking the walk. The overwhelming majority of our state governments place adoptees' OBCs under court seal and allow them to be rewritten as if the child had been naturally born to the adoptive parents. The rewritten certificate is called an *amended birth certificate.*

A birth certificate is a vital record that documents the birth of a child. The term *birth certificate* can refer to either the original document certifying the circumstances of the birth or to a certified copy or representation of the ensuing registration of that birth. Depending on the jurisdiction, a record of birth might or might not contain verification of the event by a midwife or doctor.[3]

Accordingly, an amended birth certificate is a falsified document that *changes the facts of the live birth event* and replaces the names of the child's birth parents with the names of his or her adoptive parents. In essence, this is legalized identity theft.

The original purpose of amending adoptees' OBCs was to provide privacy and protect the minor adoptee from the stigma of illegitimacy. Consider the absurdity of a protec-

---

3—"Birth Certificate," Wikipedia, accessed February 20, 2021, https://en.wikipedia.org/wiki/Birth_certificate.

tion that strips Americans of their rights so that others may think more favorably of them. Adults require no such protection, nor do adoptees of any age today, as societal norms have changed considerably regarding what constitutes "the average American family."

As of 2012, the median percentage of children born outside marriage ranges from 66 percent in Latin America to 5 percent in East Asia. In the United States and the European Union, that figure is 40 percent. The illegitimacy rate in Western societies is 1 percent to 2 percent higher if we count children who were ostensibly born to couples but were in fact covertly conceived by a different biological father.[4]

The term *illegitimate,* when referring to the birth (or existence) of any human being, must change. Adoptees are legitimate human beings and American citizens, despite the fact that our birth parents weren't married to each other when we were born. Further, we need to stop referring to adult adoptees as *adopted children*, as doing so perpetually infantilizes us in the eyes of the law. All other adults enjoy unrestricted access to their own original birth information and so should adult adoptees.

Frankly, it's insulting, as what occurred in our infancy does not and should not define us for the rest of our lives. We are emancipated American adults who were adopted as infants. There is a big difference between the rights, responsibilities, and accountabilities of adults versus those of minor children. We demand (though we shouldn't have to) equal rights and equal protection under the law as promised in the Declaration of Independence, the Constitution of the United States

---

4—"Legitimacy (family law)," Wikipedia, accessed February 20, 2021, https://en.wikipedia.org/wiki/Legitimacy_(family_law).

of America, and the Bill of Rights. We demand "liberty and justice for all."

In the forty-plus years since 1975, only ten states have fully restored the rights of adult adoptees. The fact that some adult adoptees have unrestricted access to their own information, while others do not, and the fact that the majority of adoptees are treated differently under the law than nonadoptees creates what is referred to as a *special class* of citizens who are actively being discriminated against.

While adoptees argue that placing our birth records under permanent seal and forever withholding the truth of our parentage from us is unconstitutional, others are of the opinion that those restrictions are *not* unconstitutional. The latter underscore their point by splitting hairs over language in the Declaration of Independence, the thirteenth and fourteenth amendments to the Constitution, and the Bill of Rights, arguing that adoptees are not provided for (or even referenced) in those documents, and that protections set out in those documents do not apply to adoptees or adoption.

I disagree on both counts. We are American citizens, regardless of the marital status of our birth parents at the time we were born. Further, the organized system of adoption as we know it today did not exist in the late 1700s and therefore, adoption was an unforeseen contingency. I contend that our Founding Fathers would declare, "Yes, adult adoptees are American citizens and thus entitled to the same rights and privileges, under the law, as all other Americans."

This was the unanimous opinion of America's state legislators prior to 1917, when Minnesota became the first state to pass an adoption sealed-records law.

Another point is entirely more difficult to refute: any way you slice it, the idea of an American without a heritage is simply un-American! This is the plight of millions of American adoptees—and it should not be!

Our Founding Fathers, like my cousins the former US presidents John Adams (Alden descendant, *Mayflower*) and Thomas Jefferson (Hopkins descendant, *Mayflower*), are likely rolling in their graves over the fact that many officials in power at the state level today are actively and willfully denying adult adoptees (some of whom are the Founding Father's own descendants) equal rights and protection under the law, either in part or in full, claiming to "protect us" from our "illegitimacy." I believe our Founding Fathers would discredit such officials as illegitimate, as The Declaration of Independence states:

> Governments are instituted among Men, deriving their just powers from the consent of the governed,—That whenever **any Form of Government** becomes destructive of these ends, it is the Right of the People to alter or to abolish it, and to institute new Government . . . But when a **long train of abuses and usurpations,** pursuing invariably the same Object evinces a design to reduce them under absolute Despotism, **it is their right, it is their duty, to throw off such government, and to provide new guards for their future security.**[5] [Boldface type is the author's.]

Any form of government most certainly includes state governments.

The Founding Fathers instructed that when our laws and/or those who govern us strip us of the rights they are sworn to protect and defend, that it *is our right, our duty* to abolish those laws and *install new guards* who will protect and defend our rights, to ensure our future security.

5— The Declaration of Independence, July 4, 1776, Accessed February 20, 2021, http://www.ushistory.org/declaration/document/.

The most memorable of our American presidents—the ones whose names continue to cross our lips years after they served—have been presidents who advocated in word and deed on behalf of citizens' human, civil, and/or constitutional rights. We all know who they are.

I am reminded of former President Lyndon B. Johnson, who fully emancipated African American citizens by ending segregation and removing government restrictions on their right to vote.

Some agreed with the decision to end segregation but wanted to "gradually emancipate" African Americans by continuing to withhold their voting rights as American citizens. President Johnson took a stand and decided to advocate for both at a time when it was unpopular among many people (including his own constituents) to do so. During one speech at the tail end of his campaign for re-election, Johnson shouted, "It's the right thing to do!"

His personal convictions compelled him to shout that statement even though he was almost certain that doing so would cost him the election. To his surprise, America cheered him, elected him, and was proud to follow his lead. All the way, LBJ!

My eldest half sister, Rohana, was the first to share the details of my heritage with me. She told me that I'm a thirteenth-generation American on our maternal grandmother's side and a *Mayflower* descendant (via fourteen passengers, including John Alden and Priscilla Mullins). She told me that I am a distant cousin to six US presidents (John Adams, Thomas Jefferson, John Quincy Adams, Franklin D. Roosevelt, George Bush, and George W. Bush) and one first lady (Barbara Pierce Bush). She told me that I am a descendant of Revolutionary War patriots Pvt. Edward Byram, Pvt. Isaac Lucas and Capt.

Walter McKinnie and of the Reverend Peter Prudden, one of Milford, Connecticut's, founders and the first minister Milford's First Church. In 2008, I joined the Daughters of the American Revolution (DAR).

Having studied the history of my ancestors and read their writings, I'm certain they would find the practice of withholding *any* person's true identity and heritage a grave injustice and would frown upon and rise up against any person or government that would take away any such freedom from their descendants. In fact, those values are what brought them (and many of our ancestors) here. It was woven into the very fabric of who they were.

It was important to our Founding Fathers to be recognized and remembered for their part in the forming of our great nation. They knew that theirs were the backs upon which the rest of us would step to realize *our dreams* of liberty and freedom. **This is their great legacy and ours to protect.**

Every American today has ancestors who risked everything to come here, regardless of what boat they sailed on or what year they arrived. It is one of many common threads that unite us.

The *Mayflower* Pilgrims were warned by their minister, John Carver, that it would be their descendants, not they, who would realize the dream of freedom of religion (the subject of our First Amendment). He warned them of the likelihood they'd die at sea, by starvation, or at the hands of the American Indians. *They went anyway.* They considered it "divine providence." One hundred and fifty-six years later, when we filed for divorce from England by declaring ourselves a free nation, we were warned that the British were coming, and the revolution would fail because we would be outnumbered three to one.

We were. We fought *anyway*. We won.

Our Founding Fathers' traditions included authoring or commissioning family genealogies, leaving behind funds to their churches to maintain stained-glass windows or pews bearing the family name or coat of arms, with stipulations that their names be echoed and their souls be prayed for by the congregation in perpetuity.

People operate from intention. These are not the actions of people who would condone any person being stripped of his or her heritage, nor would they support the idea of remaining forever unknown to their descendants.

The reason I've shared this history is to underscore why there is no doubt in my mind as to what our Founding Fathers intended for us or what they would say or do if they were here to advise us. They already have, in both word and deed. But most states have either forgotten or willfully ignored them.

OUR DNA—OUR INALIENABLE RIGHT

We hold these truths to be self-evident, that all men are created equal, that they are endowed by their Creator with certain inalienable rights, that among these are our DNA— the road map to the truth of our heritage.

—Geraldine Berger

I believe that the right to our birth information is implied in the Declaration of Independence by virtue of the fact that we were endowed by our Creator with our DNA, which is **the road map to our heritage.** Some of the same folks who argue that it does not violate the Constitution to withhold birth information from adoptees also contend that it was not our Creator's intention for us to know our origins. I believe there is evidence to the contrary.

The truth of our origins is in our DNA. We inherit 50 percent of our DNA from each of our parents, who inherit 50 percent of their DNA from each of their parents, and so on. As such, our DNA contains a record of our ancestry—our heritage. It exists in our cells from before our birth and can be found in our bones thousands of years after our passing. It is our natural, inalienable right. Essentially, we are inseparable from the truth of our heritage.

It is our basic, inalienable human right to know the truth of our parentage and ancestry. Our Creator has bestowed this everlasting gift upon us. So, the question is: Who among us should be able to overrule our Creator by stripping American adult adoptees of our inalienable rights and discriminating against us by denying us access to our own original birth certificates (OBCs)?

* * *

Discovering my heritage was both healing and liberating—not to mention a personal victory against New York State. I can't imagine that anyone wants to pitted against their home state in a fight for something that rightfully and literally belongs to them, and no one else. We want to feel good about our home states, and not as if our governors are the enemy—the sort who continue to strip us of our rights versus protecting them.

I continue to fight the fight by writing and speaking on this topic, because millions of other adoptees continue to suffer at the hands of the forty states and Washington, D.C., that still don't allow unrestricted access to our OBCs. No one should have to go through what I did to find out who they are and from whom they descend. It is a basic human need to know, and it is our basic human right to know.

Since 2007, inspired by my ancestors and my desire to help others experience the joy and liberation that comes with discovering the truth of their origins, I've been an adoptee rights activist. I am the administrator of several adoption community-related Facebook groups, and a professional genetic genealogist, specializing in helping adult adoptees and others with unknown parentage find their birth parents and other members of their families of origin.

I *was* an "adopted child." I *am now* an adoptee rights activist, truth seeker, and professional genetic genealogist. It's in my blood to protect and defend what I believe is right, good, and true. Now this is my quest. I hope it is yours, too.

Find out what you can do to support existing legislative efforts in the state of your birth/adoption and get involved by visiting the American Adoption Congress website: https://www.americanadoptioncongress.org/.

THE WALL OF FAME

This page provides a visual representation of the states that provide adult American adoptees with unrestricted access to their own original birth certificates (OBCs) as of January 2021.

Unrestricted Access to OBCs
Alabama
Alaska (never imposed restrictions)
*Colorado
Hawaii
Kansas (never imposed restrictions)
Maine
New Hampshire
New York
Oregon
Rhode Island

*Colorado makes the Wall of Fame even though its legislation was not a "clean" win for adoptees. The current adoption law gave birth parents the chance to block release of their surrendered children's OBCs—as long as the request to deny access to eligible parties was filed by January 1, 2016. Since no one filed that request before the deadline, adoptees have unrestricted access to their original birth certificates in Colorado.[6]

6—Geraldine Berger, "Colorado: Access to OBCs and Non-ID," The Genetic Genealogy Coach, Accessed March 3, 2021, https://www.geneticgenealogycoach.com/adoptee-colorado-obc.

THE WALL OF SHAME

The purpose of this page is to provide a visual representation of the states that (as of January 2021) *do not* provide American adult adoptees with unrestricted access to their own original birth certificates (OBCs). I call it "The Wall of Shame," to create awareness that these states continue to allow antiquated and discriminatory laws to stand, rather than *protecting* adult American adoptees and their rights by restoring their access to their own original birth information.

Discriminatory Restrictions Apply	Discriminatory Court Order Required
Arkansas	Arizona
Connecticut	California
Delaware	Florida
Illinois	Georgia
Indiana	Idaho
Maryland	Iowa
Massachusetts	Kentucky
Michigan	Louisiana
Minnesota	Mississippi
Missouri	Nevada
Nebraska	New Mexico
*New Jersey	North Carolina
Ohio	North Dakota
Pennsylvania	South Carolina
Oklahoma	Texas
South Dakota	Utah
Tennessee	Virginia
Vermont	Washington, D.C.
Washington	West Virginia
Wisconsin	Wyoming

Unrestricted access for most adoptees effective January 2017, except for 550 adoptees whose birth parents filed disclosure vetoes resulting in redaction of identifying information on the OBC.[7] While the law benefits most, it discriminates against 550 adoptees.

7—Geraldine Berger, "New Jersey: Access to OBCs and Non-ID," The Genetic Genealogy Coach, Accessed March 1, 2021, https://www.geneticgenealogycoach.com/adoptee-new-jersey-obc.

PART 4

Your Journey to Living in the Know

8

Getting Started with the Berger Method

There are many ways to approach your journey to living in the know. Whether your journey began years ago, or you are just getting started, I recommend reading this section in its entirely, as there may be important steps that you did not know about or have otherwise skipped.

THREE BILLION PAIRS OF RUBY SLIPPERS

DNA testing is the most effective way to get around the restrictive and discriminatory laws and family secrets that separate adoptees and others with unknown parentage from their own original identities. Approximately three billion base pairs (the bases are adenine, thymine, guanine, and cytosine) comprise the human genome . . . our DNA! I like to refer to these babies as our "three billion pairs of ruby slippers" because just like Dorothy's ruby slippers in *The Wizard of Oz*, they can take us home.

To simplify the search process, I have developed the

acronym RONDA to describe the steps. (**R**egistries, **O**riginal Birth Certificate, **N**on-ID, **D**NA Testing, **A**sk for Help.) I will describe each step on the following pages.

It is important to note that the steps can be taken out of order. In fact, I recommend that if you have not yet begun and are interested in getting started quickly, order an AncestryDNA test from www.ancestry.com first. *Then* return to reading this section of the book.

Ancestry.com currently offers three different DNA test kits with various features. You may order any of them, as they all include "Origins and Ethnicity" and "DNA Matches," but the basic AncestryDNA test kit will suffice. As of 2021, the regular cost of this kit is $99, however, Ancestry.com runs sales throughout the year, and you can purchase a kit for as little as $59, usually preceding major holidays.

While there are many DNA tests on the market today, I recommend taking the AncestryDNA test first—yes, it matters—for several reasons that I will address later.

Pause now to order your AncestryDNA test.

The DNA test kit will take three to five days to arrive, during which time you can get back to the book. (Note: I am not compensated by any of the DNA testing companies or third-party tools for DNA analysis (such as GEDmatch) to provide information or review products and services mentioned here or on my website, www.geneticgenealogycoach.com. Any product or service mentioned should be researched directly through the manufacturer or provider.)

There are actually more than five steps involved in an adoption search. But this *Quick-Start Guide* highlights the quick and relatively simple things you can do before engaging my services (or those of another) or making contact with your families of origin.

R IS FOR REGISTRIES (ADOPTION REUNION REGISTRIES)

Adoption reunion registries exist to help reunite adoptees with members of their families of origin—most often their birth mothers. They are referred to as *voluntary mutual-consent registries*, where adult adoptees (over the age of eighteen) and birth mothers and/or members of adoptees' birth families can independently register, with the hope of being reunited. "Matches" are made through these registries using the adoptee's date of birth, location of birth, and other details.

Reunions through the registries are made possible provided that both the adoptee and the biological family member(s) have registered with the same entity and have agreed—usually via a consent form or consent portion of the registration form—to freely share identifying information, such as their current names and contact information, with one another. While all registries allow adoptees' birth mothers to register, some registries do not allow other family members (i.e., siblings, aunts, uncles, grandparents, etc.) to do so.

Some registries are state-run, while others are nonprofit or commercial (for-profit) entities. Most state-run registries are managed by the Department of Health in the state of the adoptee's birth and/or adoption, and there is no cost to register. Some adoptees were born in one state and adopted in another. In those instances, I recommend contacting both states and registering in both state registries, if possible.

For links to the adoption registries by state, visit my website (www.geneticgenealogycoach.com), go to *Adoptee Records* on the main navigation bar, and select *Adoption Reunion Registries by State* from the drop-down menu.

I highly recommend that adoptees participate in the adoption registry in the state in which they were born and/or adopted in addition to the following two nonprofit registries: ALMA (www.almasociety.org) and the International Soundex Reunion Registry (www.isrr.org).

ALMA and ISRR are the two oldest and largest adoption reunion registries in the United States.

In recent years, many online adoption reunion registries have emerged, some touting themselves as the largest, best, etc. Participation in these registries is usually free, and some are managed by individual adoptees or birth parents who hope to find *their* missing person.

While some truth seekers have had success going this route, the continuous emergence of these online registries fragments the adoptee/birth parent community, thereby lessening participants' chances of finding a match—unless every adoptee and birth parent registers in the same registry or in all registries.

Also, it is important to know specifically who is managing the registry and what qualifies them to do so and to understand what will happen to your confidential registration information should the online registry become defunct or suddenly disappear.

In the interest of making more reunions possible via adoption reunion registries, I recommend that adoptees and birth parents who are searching for one another participate in their relevant state registries, ALMA, and ISRR. I also recommend that others in the online adoption community direct adoptees and birth parents to these registries first and foremost.

O IS FOR ORIGINAL BIRTH CERTIFICATE (OBC)

Adult adoptees in ten of the fifty states are granted unrestricted access to what is called an "unofficial copy" of their original birth certificate, without redactions. What makes the copy unofficial is that it doesn't bear a raised seal and cannot be used for legal identification purposes. "Without redactions" means that the name the mother used at the time of the birth will appear in the "mother's maiden name" field of the original birth certificate. In forty of the fifty states and Washington, D.C., restrictions and/or redactions apply.

For links to information on the laws governing adult adoptees' access to their own original birth certificates by state, visit my website (www.geneticgenealogycoach.com), go to *Adoptee Records* on the main navigation bar, and select *OBCs and Non-ID by State* from the drop-down menu. For a quick view of adoptee access to their OBCs by state, be sure to see the pie graph located at the bottom of that webpage or read the The Wall of Fame and The Wall of Shame in chapter 7.

It is sometimes helpful but not essential to the success of your search to have a copy of your OBC. Most birth mothers will have married and changed their names (some several times) since they surrendered an infant for adoption; and others, like my birth mother, used an alias. Some may have common names, making it nearly impossible to identify and/or locate the correct person. Also, the home address listed on the OBC may have been your birth mother's place of residence at the time of her pregnancy and not the address of her family home.

If you are able to easily send for a copy of your OBC, I recommend doing so. Processing times vary from state to state; it can take weeks or months to receive your OBC. If you are not able to order your OBC easily, don't worry about it.

N IS FOR NONIDENTIFYING INFORMATION (NON-ID)

Nonidentifying information (aka non-ID) is information about your birth parents that was probably gathered by a social worker (or another assigned professional) via interview(s) with your birth mother during her pregnancy. It is standard practice for this information to be included as a permanent part of the adoption file. It may include information such as details about your birth parents' appearance, scholastics, hobbies and interests, heath history, personalities, the profession(s) of their parents, the number of siblings they had at the time and their ages, etc.

It's called "nonidentifying," as when it is prepared for release to you (upon your request), names and addresses are not included.

Even though non-ID is information about the birth parent(s), adoptees often refer to it as "my non-ID," as they must request it, it is about *their* birth parent(s), and it is prepared and released to *them*. Those who help guide adoptees in their search will ask them, "Have you sent for your non-ID?"

Sometimes nonidentifying information is scant. You may only be given information about your birth mother's hair and eye color, height, religion, and age at the time of your birth. Your biological father may be listed as "unknown."

There doesn't seem to be any correlation between the amount of nonidentifying information provided and who arranged the adoption, an adoption agency or private attorney.

Nonidentifying information can also be false, as it reflects what the birth mother knew, shared, or chose to be truthful about with the interviewer. It is also possible that the interviewer might have deliberately omitted or changed information to ensure that the parties would never be able to identify one another. In fact, this practice was quite common for adoptions that took place during the Baby Scoop Era. I was born in 1965 and my adoption was a *private adoption* (conducted via an attorney specializing in adoptions versus an adoption agency). The nonidentifying information that I received from the New York State Department of Health in the early 1990s stated that both of my birth parents had brown hair and brown eyes, both were minors, and both were of the Jewish faith. As I would later discover, some of this information was erroneous. My birth mother was raised in the Methodist faith, my biological father was raised in the Catholic faith, and he was not a minor at the time I was conceived.

Nonidentifying information about your birth parents may be requested from the state in which you were born and/or adopted. It may also be requested from the adoption agency, if it is still in business or if you are able to find out who now owns those records and whether or not that entity provides such a service. For information on to how to request your non-ID, visit my website at www.geneticgenealogycoach.com, go to *Adoptee Records* on the main navigation bar, and select *OBCs and Non-ID by State* from the drop-down menu.

If the non-ID information is true, it can become essential to identifying an adoptee's birth parents when used in conjunction with DNA testing.

For example, if an adoptee I'm working with has the results of a DNA test, I will eventually identify the immediate families of that person's birth parents (that is, the birth parents' siblings and parents). If I discover that the birth mother was one of four daughters, all of whom were close in age and unmarried at the time of the adoptee's birth, but I know from the non-ID that she had blond hair, was five foot five, was the second child born to her parents, played the flute, and planned to go to secretarial school, that *nonidentifying* information becomes *identifying*.

Likewise, if the biological father was one of several sons, but I know from the nonidentifying information that he was five foot ten with hazel eyes and played varsity soccer in high school and served in the US Airforce, then I'll be able to identify him (versus his brothers) as the biological father.

D IS FOR DNA TESTING

If you watch television, you are likely aware that companies like Ancestry, 23andMe, and MyHeritage offer DNA tests to the consumer market at reasonable prices and that people around the world are using them to discover their ancestral homelands and ethnicities, which sometimes come as a surprise. What the companies do not publicize in the ads is the fact that when you submit your DNA sample, each company will pair you with your genetic "matches" (aka relatives) and deposit them into approximate categories of relationship, based on how many identical segments of DNA that you and your matches share and inherited from your common ancestors. So, you not only receive a breakdown of your ethnic mix—where in the world your ancestors probably lived—but you are also provided with a long list of "DNA matches" or "DNA relatives" (depending on the testing company). They are your biological family members.

DNA Doesn't Lie ... People Do

Some individuals question the validity of DNA testing, especially when they review their list of DNA matches and find names of individuals they do not recognize among their closest matches—from "close family" down to the "third cousin" category. They believe that they already know all of their relatives to this degree of relation and that if a name appears that they do not recognize, it must mean that their DNA results are inaccurate. This is especially true of *late-discovery adoptees* (LDAs) and the nonadopted (either with or without known paternity).

When individuals with known parentage encounter DNA matches whose names they don't recognize, the latter are usually adoptees or others with unknown parentage. DNA matching is based on finding identical DNA segments between testers. DNA matches are *not* made based on family tree information provided by testers or their matches; they are made based on identical DNA segments only. This is a point of confusion for some novices.

One's genetic matches, within the aforementioned relationship categories, are, in fact, one's genetic relatives. Some of these DNA matches may use screen names versus their real names, and some may or may not link their DNA results to their family tree online (if the testing company provides that feature).

Some people who link their DNA results to a family tree may have errors in their family trees. Perhaps, for example, they have misattributed their line of descent to a person who shares the same name but who is *not* their ancestor. The family trees of people who do not yet know they were adopted will include the names of their adoptive parents and *their* ancestors, and a genetic relative may struggle to understand through which family line they are related, as there does not appear to be one.

Researchers often assume the family trees of their genetic relatives are correct. This is a faulty assumption that can derail DNA adoption searches and/or family tree research. Many of the cases I work on require me to correct the trees of my clients' DNA matches to find the correct connections.

Some people claim, "I would know if my mother/father, sister/brother, aunt/uncle or cousin gave up a baby for adoption. We're a close family." Based on my experience, however, it is more likely that one would *not* know.

It's worth noting that there *can* be false positives in DNA matching, and these are most typically found between distant matches who appear in each other's fourth- to eighth-cousin categories. One way this can occur is when two or more testers' share DNA segments are *identical by state* (IBS), versus *identical by descent* (IBD).

Generally speaking, DNA segments that are IBS are segments that are coincidentally identical between two or more individuals and not usually indicative of a recent common ancestor; they are typically very small segments shared by many people, in a given population or between populations. DNA segments that are IBD are identical segments between two or more individuals, that are inherited and can usually be traced to a recent common ancestor.

Small segments under 6 centimorgans are almost always IBS, with a 1 percent chance of being a legitimate match, whereas with segments longer than 6 centimorgans, it is more likely that the segments are identical because of a common ancestor. Large segments, longer than 45 centimorgans, occur among matches that almost always have a common ancestor within recent generations. In these cases, the statistical odds of being IBS are insignificant; you can hang your hat on them.

But that is *way* more than you need to know right now, or possibly ever. Essentially, if you have DNA matches who are categorized as third cousins or closer, you can be sure that they are, in fact, your genetic relatives.

Sometimes a DNA match may appear in a relationship category that is either closer or more distant than it is in actuality.

This can and does occur for different reasons. For example, second cousins whose common set of great-grandparents were related to each other (cousins marrying cousins) share more DNA in common than second cousins whose great-grandparents were *not* related to each another. As a result, they may appear in a closer relationship category than second cousins whose great-grandparents were *not* related to each other, who will most likely appear within the correct category.

On the other hand, half second cousins may appear in the third-cousin category, as they only share *one* great-grandparent in common and therefore less DNA than second cousins who share *two* great-grandparents in common. Keep in mind that DNA-matching systems consider the amount of identical DNA segments testers have in common *only* and deposit matches into *approximate* relationship categories accordingly. Also, it can be confusing, even for professional genetic genealogists, to predict whether a close relative is a half sibling, an aunt or uncle, a niece or nephew, grandparent, grandchild, or double first cousin since all share the same approximate amount of DNA in common. The same holds true for great-grandparents/great-grandchildren, great aunts/uncles/nieces/ nephews, half aunts/uncles/nieces/nephews, half first cousins and first cousins. The list goes on, but the important takeaway is that within specific shared DNA ranges, different *actual* relationships are possible—the exception being parent/child relationships—regardless of the fact that one's matches appear in certain relationship categories. The system is making its best guess based on empirical data (the relationship that is most commonly verified between testers sharing a certain amount of DNA in common). But the guess may be incorrect. Other information, such as a match's age, if known, or that person's proximity of relationship to another DNA relative can help determine the exact relationship. These are but a few of the nuances that frustrate the novice and that can lead to false assumptions regarding the identity of one's birth parents.

When you submit your DNA sample, your DNA is compared with *reference panels* comprised of hundreds of thousands of DNA samples from people who have proven ancestral ties to particular parts of the world, usually over several hundred years. Those connections are verified via family tree research.

Your ethnicity estimates are produced using sophisticated algorithms that compare your DNA to those whose DNA has been used to form the reference panels. People whose ancestors hail from a particular part of the world will share more DNA in common than those who are from different regions. These estimates give us an idea of where our ancestors may have lived. Your ethnicity estimates will vary, depending on where you test or which service is analyzing your DNA data, as their reference panels vary. In addition, the DNA testing companies compare your DNA to the DNA of millions of other testers and use algorithms to determine your approximate relationship to them (if any) based on the number of identical DNA segments you share in common; these are your DNA matches/relatives.

It is important to mention that it's possible for third cousins and more distant cousins to share no DNA in common, which is accounted for by genetic recombination. This phenomenon is often discovered when two full or half siblings who have DNA tested have a third cousin who has also tested, and that cousin appears as a DNA match to only one of the siblings and not the other. Or that match may appear as a third cousin to one of the siblings and a more distant cousin to the other.

We each inherit 50 percent of our DNA from our mothers and 50 percent from our fathers. This means that there is another 50 percent of each parent's DNA that we did not inherit from them, and by extension their ancestors. When you have children, they will have 50 percent of your DNA and 50 percent of your partner's DNA and *approximately* 25 percent of their grandparents' DNA, as DNA is inherited in chunks that are not exact in size.

The DNA of our ancestors *approximately* halves itself in each subsequent generation, which accounts for how it is possible for third cousins (who share a common set of second great-grandparents) to share no DNA in common. This is more common among fourth cousins and more distant cousins, although it sometimes does occur among third cousins. This is also why only about 80 percent of your fourth to sixth cousins, who have DNA tested and can prove a paper-trail connection to ancestors in common with you, will appear among your matches, while about 20 percent of them will not.

DNA Adoption Search

The term "DNA Adoption Search" means adoptees using DNA testing as a means of identifying their birth parents and/ or other genetic relatives.

Those who are new to truth seeking may not know that autosomal DNA (atDNA) testing, offered by companies like AncestryDNA, 23andMe, FamilyTreeDNA, and MyHeritage can be their "yellow brick road" to success or that their DNA samples are their "ruby slippers"—the magic or power they've had all along to find their way back to Kansas—metaphorically, their origins.

Your journey will have twists and turns and forks in the road—almost all of them do—and there may be times when all seems hopeless. You may even encounter a few "flying monkeys" who are committed to keeping the truth of your origins a secret.

Adoptions in the United States during the Baby Scoop Era were fraught with lies, secrecy, and corruption *on top of* the unwillingness of most states to provide adult adoptees with unrestricted access to their own original birth information. Adoptees and others with unknown parentage love DNA, because DNA doesn't lie. It just is what it is. You either share a certain number of identical segments of DNA in common with another individual (who also independently tested) or you don't.

Thanks to DNA testing, it is now possible for adoptees and others with unknown parentage to *do something* to put their lifelong preoccupation of their own original birth identity to rest. It has changed the fates of adoptees and other persons with unknown parentage around the world. Thanks to DNA testing, many of us are now living in the know.

For the adoptee who knows none of his genetic family members, every person on his DNA match list is a relative he never knew. It is difficult to fathom that after a lifetime of *not knowing* who your genetic relatives are, that within four to six weeks, you will see a list of hundreds and potentially thousands of your relatives. In this way, DNA testing is rendering the discriminatory laws of the forty states and Washington, D.C. ineffectual. Our DNA is the cypher containing information about our parentage and heritage, and DNA testing is the tool to help us decode it.

While DNA testing is a great tool for many adoptees and others with unknown parentage (predominately those who were born in the United States and whose ancestors, in recent generations, were also born here) it is not a miracle path or solution for everyone. Some ethnic groups are underrepresented in the DNA pools. The fewer the people who get tested from a particular ethnic group, the lower the statistical odds of individuals from that group receiving relatively close DNA matches (up to third cousins).

In my own search for my biological father, it was over three years before I received a close enough DNA match/relative to identify him. He was half Italian and half Croatian, and both of those ethnic groups are underrepresented in the DNA pools. As such, for several years, my DNA matches were distant (fourth to eighth cousins)—too distant to solve the mystery.

The issue in this type of case is that ancestors whom the tester has in common with her distant DNA matches were born hundreds of years ago (in my case, in the mid-1700s) making it difficult to build a family tree without missing some individuals—and therefore, potentially entire family lines of descent. Also, the family tree, which contains thousands of individuals, is far too large. And by extension, there will be far too many candidates—scores or even hundreds—for birth parents in the correct generation, even if it were possible to capture every line of descent.

It has been my experience that in cases like mine, closer matches usually do come along, but it can take weeks, months, or years. Unfortunately, this is less common for foreign-born adoptees (i.e., those born in Eastern Europe, Asia, Central or South America, etc.) or those with unknown parentage whose parents were born abroad and never emigrated to the United States. In those instances, DNA testing is not very useful in solving cases of unknown parentage. This may change as DNA testing is offered in more countries.

All of these wrinkles render searches far more difficult and even unsolvable until closer matches present.

I encourage everyone I know to DNA test and to give DNA tests as gifts. Will you? It is fun to discover where in the world your ancestors came from, and it helps adoptees and others with unknown parentage to discover the truth of their origins. As the number of people in the DNA pools increases, so do the odds of all of us receiving closer DNA matches, which is precisely what adoptees and others with unknown parentage need in order to discover the truth of their origins.

DNA Testing Strategy

I first published my step-by-step proven DNA testing strategy on my website (www.geneticgenealogycoach), in 2014 and have continued to share it widely in adoption community groups and on social media. Since then, newbies, volunteers, other authors, and professionals alike have adopted my strategy as their own. I'm glad to see that it has finally taken hold and that my years of hard work are benefitting adoptees and others with unknown parentage. It is my hope that you, too, will share my strategy with others. If you do so in writing, please credit the author. There are many autosomal DNA testing companies and new ones continue to emerge to grab a share of the market.

The Big Four

The "Big Four" DNA testing companies are Ancestry, 23andMe, FamilyTreeDNA, and MyHeritage, in that order. These four companies have the greatest number of testers/members in their respective DNA databases (aka "DNA pools").

It is best to be in all Big Four DNA pools, as you never know where your closest DNA matches/relatives have tested, and close matches (third cousins or closer) are essential to identifying one's birth parents. "Fishing in more ponds" increases the statistical odds of finding closer matches/relatives. That said, it is only actually necessary to test with two of the four companies.

All of the Big Four allow you to download your "Raw DNA Data" from their websites, once your DNA results have populated to your online account(s). Your raw DNA data is series of electronic files containing alleles that make up your DNA. The files come in a ZIP folder. The data is uploaded intact, as a ZIP folder, to other sites or analysis programs that offer the feature.

Ancestry and 23andMe *do not* accept competitor uploads. This means that you may test with those companies and download your raw DNA data, however, you *cannot* upload your raw DNA data from *other* (competing) testing companies, to their sites.

Conversely, FamilyTreeDNA and MyHeritage *do* allow competitor uploads. This eliminates the need to purchase test kits through their companies. You may opt to pay a small one-time fee to unlock certain DNA features and/or tools on their sites, but the cost of doing so is far less than purchasing another test kit or an ongoing subscription. This keeps the cost of testing down while allowing you to fish in the Big Four ponds.

Here Is My DNA-Testing Strategy

1. **Test with AncestryDNA** *first*. I can't stress this enough. AncestryDNA is the largest DNA pool, with (as of 2021) approximately twenty million members, many of whom have extensive family trees, which are essential to a successful search.

Experienced volunteers usher all adoptees and birth parents here first to increase the odds of finding a parent/child match with their first test. **That said, it is best to be in all of the "Big Four" DNA pools.**

2. **Download your AncestryDNA raw data to your computer.** Save the zip file to your desktop so it's easy to locate, and do not open/unzip it or extract files. (See chapter 10 for detailed instructions.)

3. **Create a free FamilyTreeDNA account and upload your AncestryDNA raw data** via free autosomal transfer. Consider upgrading your membership for a minimal one-time fee to unlock all Family Finder features (optional). This saves time and money versus having to purchase another DNA test and wait for results. (See chapter 10 for detailed instructions.)

4. **Create a free MyHeritage account and upload your Ancestry raw data** (via free autosomal transfer). Consider upgrading for a minimal one-time fee to unlock all site features (optional). This saves time and money versus having to purchase another DNA test and wait for results. (See chapter 10 for detailed instructions.)

5. **Create a free GEDmatch account and upload your AncestryDNA raw data.** GEDmatch is a third-party electronic utility and DNA data analyzer, *not* a DNA testing company. Members can upload their DNA raw data from any of the major testing companies (for free), potentially increasing the number of DNA matches/relatives that turn up. People may find matches they would not have encountered otherwise. (See chapter 10 for detailed instructions.)

6. **Test with 23andMe, if necessary.** If your matches are close enough, you may not need to test here. If you'd like to test anyway, go ahead, but only after you have tested with AncestryDNA. I encourage

adoptees and those with unknown parentage to get into all of the DNA pools, though this may not be necessary to solve your case. For those who have already tested with 23andMe, I include instructions on how to download your raw DNA data in chapter 10. You may upload this raw DNA data to FamilyTreeDNA, MyHeritage, and GEDmatch.com.

A IS FOR ASK FOR HELP

Solving cases of unknown parentage via DNA testing and genetic genealogy is somewhat of an art. The learning curve is steep, and it is not a hard science with set formulas, which if applied correctly, will provide the correct solution.

Many people do not have the time or inclination to go it alone, and there are dangers in doing so, such as identifying the wrong people as one's birth parent(s) or worse, making communication missteps that close the door permanently between themselves and particular members of their family (or families) of origin. Having been a member of the adoption search community for over thirty years, I do not recommend going it alone.

Search Angels

The majority of adoptees who join mutual-consent reunion registries, such as ALMA, are advised to DNA test if it turns out their birth mother (or other family member) is not in the registry. Adoptees who join online forums and other groups are similarly advised. But when their DNA results are in, most do not know what to do or who to turn to next.

Volunteers in the adoption community are called "search angels." Some are knowledgeable and helpful . . . to a point. A select few are able to solve cases of unknown parentage using an adoptee's DNA test results, particularly when one's genetic matches are very close (parents, siblings, half siblings, and first cousins).

I caution adoptees just beginning to search for their families of origin to vet any volunteer carefully, as it has become popular in online forums for people without any experience or track record to refer to themselves as search angels. These well-meaning individuals are usually other adoptees who know the initial steps and take a personal interest in your case, creating hope. One problem is that they often lose interest when they get stuck.

Some volunteers create a bigger problem when they try to act as the intermediary between adoptees and their genetic family members. When they initially call the family member, they often rely on excerpts of scripts from television shows that reunite adoptees with their families of origin. Such scripts almost guarantee what I call "permanent hang-ups" when used in real life. Television scripts play to the cameras for dramatic effect, but in real life, they can shake birth parents to their cores, particularly those who have never shared their secret with anyone. Such scripts do not consider who else may be in the room with the call recipient at the time of the call, nor do they consider the approach, the words, or other factors, all of which matter. Sometimes the term "birth mother" alone is enough to draw a verbal threat followed by abrupt hang-up.

For example: "I have no idea who you are, what you're talking about, or how you got my number, but you better never call here again, or I'll report you and your number to the police!" Click.

Also, in real life, neither volunteers nor professionals go to the home of a birth parent or other genetic family member of the adoptee. When the adoptee does this herself, it is an approach known as "door-stepping" in the adoption community.

Some adoptees harbor the fantasy of appearing on their birth mother's doorstep out of the blue and ringing the doorbell, and a small percentage of adoptees actually do it. But I advise strongly against it, as it almost never works out the way the adoptee hopes it will.

In sum, vet any volunteers and know that just because someone says she is a search angel, it may be that she just *wants* to be one. Be sure to ask how many cases she has solved. Ask for references and verify them before working together. Ask her to agree *not* to make contact with your genetic family members unless she is an experienced intermediary. Your search, the length of time it will take, whether or not the correct results will be achieved, and the possibility of contact with genetic family members depend on it.

Hire a Professional

Professional genetic genealogists typically have greater success solving cases of unknown parentage than volunteers do. Ideally, that professional (a) is an adoptee as I am and (b) has experience acting as an intermediary between adoptees and their birth parents or other genetic family members.

Working with an experienced intermediary is key. Those without real expertise may inadvertently sabotage any chance of reunion between an adoptee and his or her birth parent(s), as those calls can be emotional minefields. Knowing how to navigate them, versus winging it or following the example of television scripts, is often the difference between a successful and an unsuccessful first contact—and in some cases, any future contact.

My mentors in intermediary services are birth mothers who surrendered children for adoption in the 1950s, 1960s, and 1970s. Some were pioneers of the Adoption Reform Movement. As a result, I intimately understand the thoughts and feelings of those who have surrendered their children for adoption, their reactions to first contact (whether or not they themselves were actively searching or ever have), what to say, how to say it, and what not to say. An experienced intermediary gives birth parents the emotional space to process their feelings and the fact that their adult child has been searching for them and is interested in contact.

Mistakes to Avoid

Some adoptees begin initiating contact with their DNA matches/relatives immediately, in an effort to solicit help in solving their case. They begin with the fact that they are an adoptee in search of their birth parents and tell their story, asking for help in solving the mystery. I advise against this approach, as it can close doors quickly. Some of your DNA matches/relatives may not want to get involved in helping you discover which of their family members is your birth parent. They are not comfortable with the idea of "outing" a family member as your birth parent. They don't want to let on to your birth parent that they now know his or her secret and may quickly sour others in the family on your existence and research goals. You may discover that the family tree linked to that person's DNA account has been locked or otherwise removed from view, and the same holds true for other members of the same family. This scenario tends to be more common among very close DNA matches/relatives.

Unless your DNA match/relative is your parent, sibling, half sibling, aunt, or uncle, it is unlikely that your matches/relatives will know the identity of your birth parent(s). Even aunts and uncles may have no idea which one of their siblings it could be. This scenario is more common than one would imagine. Some insist that *they would know* if their sibling conceived a child or placed a child for adoption out of wedlock. They might deny the effectiveness or veracity of DNA testing. More often than not, they *do not* know.

Contact with first, second, or third cousins about your story can lead to rapid-fire phone communication within a particular family line. A birth parent and his or her secret (the pregnancy and your birth) can be exposed to the extended family in a number of days or even hours, and birth parents usually *do not* appreciate that. They may adamantly deny their involvement and refuse to have contact with you.

I have had direct involvement in cases in which a DNA match/relative knows or suspects who the birth parent is and goes as far as to warn that person and anyone in the family who has had his or her DNA tested not to talk to the truth seeker. Further, the DNA match/relative asks family members who may be independently considering DNA testing not to do it.

Keep in mind, also, that biological fathers may have no idea that they ever fathered a child. This can be so even if your non-ID indicates otherwise, as sometimes the man a birth mother believed was the biological father was not.

I always recommend that adoptees or others with unknown parentage test with AncestryDNA first. One reason is that www.Ancestry.com provides a feature that allows members to link their family tree to their DNA results, and many people do. (Some sites do not offer this feature). The primary reason is that they have the greatest number of DNA tested members, so the statistical odds of a closer match is greater.

When your DNA results are in, I recommend that you do not immediately initiate messaging contact via Ancestry's system with any of your DNA matches/relatives. Instead, view the family trees of your closest DNA matches/relatives (up to and including the third-cousin level) and take screenshots of their family trees. You will need a paid membership to access that feature of the site.

That way, should anyone you contact choose to lock his or her family tree or remove it entirely, at least you will have a copy of it. This is the "better safe than sorry" approach. The family tree(s) may not be helpful to you per se, but the trees' contents could very well help a professional solve your mystery.

Free Phone Consultation: 1 (833) WHO-ARE-U

I offer a free phone consultation. During the consultation, prospective clients share their research goals and DNA results with me, so I can assess whether or not I can solve their mystery. If your DNA matches/relatives are (approximate) third cousins or closer, it is likely I will be able to do so.

If you are interested in contacting me, you may call the number above or get in touch via the "contact" form on my website: (www.geneticgenealogycoach.com).

Why Me?

Since 2014, I have reunited hundreds of adoptees with their birth parents and have solved many other types of cases of unknown parentage. I identified my own biological father via DNA testing and have been an active member of the adoption community since 1991 through ALMA, an organization close to my heart that reunited my birth mother and me in 2007.

I have successfully reunited many other ALMA members with birth parents who were not registered with ALMA, using DNA testing and genetic genealogy.

People find me online and via referral and speaking engagements. Each case I solve widens the lenses through which I view the next one. Many cases cannot be solved without the tacit knowledge obtained by having worked on hundreds of cases, with all the nuances they present—nuances that are not taught or published anywhere, but when considered, produce the correct conclusions.

My work is in the capacity of genetic genealogist, coach/consultant, support system, intermediary, and friend. It's personal. My clients confide in me, sharing all known details of their birth (and adoption or donor conception) information, as well as their feelings.

What separates me from other professional genetic genealogists is the fact that I am an adoptee in addition to having long-term, personal involvement and experience in the adoption search and support community as a search angel, an experienced intermediary between adoptees and their birth parents, and an adoptee rights activist. I know, firsthand, what it feels like not to know the truth of your origins, ancestry, and health history. "The need to know" was a lifelong preoccupation for me, and my search for my birth mother lasted twenty-four years.

I coach adoptees and their birth parents and/or other genetic family members through the uncharted waters of search and reunion to ensure the best possible outcomes between them. It is my pleasure and a privilege to help others discover the truth of their origins and to unite and reunite families. I look forward to hearing from you.

9

Birth Parents and other Biological Family Members

I am frequently contacted by birthmothers and other biological family members who are searching for the adoptee. They often ask if I can help them identify and locate the adoptee in the same way I help adoptees identify and locate their birth parents and other members of their families of origin.

The short answer is no. The reason is that when they DNA test, most of their relatives in the "close family" to "third cousin" categories will be known relations to them, barring occasions when the adoptee or a child of the adoptee has already tested, and in those instances the system will alert them to the "parent/child" or "close family" match, respectively. As such, they will not usually need my help determining the identity of the match.

That said, there are things that birth parents and other biological relatives of the adoptee can do to improve their chances of being found, if the adoptee is searching for them, too, and also possibly if he is not.

The steps are very similar to the Berger Method ("RONDA")

outlined and discussed in chapter 8. If the adoptee is searching for her birthmother or other birth family members, she will be directed to:

1. Register with voluntary mutual-consent registries, such as ALMA and ISRR, and perhaps some free online registries for adoptees and birth parents—and consent to be contacted should a match be made.

2. Register with the state-run mutual-consent adoption registry/registries, in the state(s) she was born and/or adopted, which is free. And consent to be contacted should a match be made.

3. Send for her nonidentifying information via the state(s) where she was born and/or adopted.

4. Take a DNA test with AncestryDNA first, as this is where all experienced volunteers usher adoptees and birth parents, to increase their chances of a match with the first test.

5. Once her DNA results are in, if there is no "parent/child" match or "close family" match, she'll be directed to expand her presence into the DNA pools (mentioned in chapter 8) to increase her chances of such a match. (Refer to chapter 10 for detailed instructions.)

For greater detail on these steps and links to the appropriate resources, see chapter 8.

WHAT YOU CAN DO

What you (members of the adoptee's families of origin) can do is to establish and maintain a presence in the same places that the adoptee is being directed to find you. The idea is for you and the adoptee to *bump into one another* in one or more of these places. The more places you both maintain a presence, the greater the statistical odds of being reunited or united, whichever is the case.

To get started:

1. Register with voluntary mutual-consent registries, such as ALMA and ISRR, and perhaps some free online registries for adoptees and birth parents. And consent to be contacted should a match be made.

2. Register with the state-run mutual-consent adoption registry/registries, in the state(s) she was born and/ or adopted, which is free—and consent to be contacted should a match be made. (For information on the state-run registries, visit my website: www.geneticgenealogycoach.com, click on *Adoptee Records* in the main navigation bar and select *Adoption Reunion Registries by State* from the drop-down menu.

   Note: *Be sure to keep your name and contact information current on all of these registries. If you change your name, move, or get a new phone number, update the appropriate registries accordingly and immediately.*

3. Purchase an AncestryDNA test and submit your DNA sample. This involves creating an account on www.Ancestry.com, where your test results will appear once your sample has been processed.

4. Once your DNA results are in, if there is no "parent/ child" or "close family" match with a name that *is not* familiar to you, expand your presence in the DNA pools (mentioned in chapter 8) to increase your chances of such a match. (Refer to chapter 10 for detailed instructions.)

IMPORTANT CONSIDERATIONS

Sometimes the adoptee you are hoping to find has been searching for you for weeks, months, years—or not at all. If the adoptee is actively searching for you, he will (most likely) be very glad to be contacted by you, either via one of the mutual-consent registries or via a private message on a DNA testing site's email system. If you are united/reunited via one of the registries, there is no mystery that you share a mutual desire for contact.

LATE-DISCOVERY ADOPTEES (LDAs)

If the adoptee was never told he was adopted, he will be confused or shocked to have received a DNA match in the "parent/child" or "close family" category and may also feel that way when contacted by a birth parent or other close family member who reaches out explaining the biological connection. He may question the validity of his DNA test results, you, and your reason for contacting him, and he may become very upset as he plunges into a state of cognitive dissonance, denial, or both. He will recover from this emotional upset, but expect it to take some time.

Despite your good intentions, his reality has just been shaken—by you. He has just discovered that the family narrative he was told and believed may be false. He is not convinced.

In these instances, the adoptee's emotional reflex is to believe the narrative, not you. He may become defensive (this is common) and tell you why you're wrong and that he knows *for a fact* that what you have just told him is not true and can't be true. Do not argue with him or become defensive; it's not about you. He is a late-discovery adoptee (LDA), and the "facts" he was told are lies. He is in denial, the first stage of an LDA's experience when he hears the truth. This is normal and it passes—in time. How long? Everyone is different. But eventually he will realize the truth, as the new information often spurs a personal research process, during which time the adoptee simultaneously moves through the steps outlined in the Kubler-Roth stages of death and dying, which are also pertinent to other life experiences. They are: denial, anger, bargaining, depression, acceptance—and he may not necessarily experience them in that order. Late-discovery adoptees often benefit from support in the form of counseling to cope with issues of identity crisis (they are not biologically who they thought they were) and unresolved feelings of anger toward their parents, who withheld the truth from them. This is especially true of LDAs whose parents have passed away. In such cases, the adoptee will never be able to confront them with the truth and have his questions answered, the main question being, "Why didn't you tell me the truth?"

It is not your job to be his counselor. He needs a safe and private space to address all he's going through, and you're not the appropriate person to offer it; you are the person who just rocked his world. You must back off and let him come to you. He may or may not, however, any other action on your part, at this juncture, is unwelcome and will most likely destroy your chances for future contact. When the LDA has reached "acceptance," he will have questions, which will likely spur his desire to resume contact.

The adoptee may have originally DNA tested to confirm what he believed about his family history, to learn more about it, or because he had suspicions that he was privately hoping to annul or confirm for himself.

He may have tested in the hopes of identifying and locating biological family members, or it's possible he received the DNA test as a gift and had no prior interest in DNA testing. The bottom line is . . . there is no way to know.

Some birth parents and other biological family members are trepidatious of initiating contact, fearful that they will be the one to inform the adoptee that he was adopted, if he was never told so by his adoptive parents.

CASES OF UNKNOWN PARENTAGE

Sometimes your biological relative is *not* an adoptee. She may have been raised by her biological mother, and her father who raised her is not her biological father. In rare cases, the situation is reversed, and the child is raised by her biological father and his wife, who is not the child's mother. (See Verne Albright's story, in chapter 11).

Whichever is the case, it may be unknown to her until later in life—or until you find one another in the same DNA pool. If so, she may react similarly to LDAs when she notices and/ or is contacted by a birth parent or other close family member. Sometimes she and her father are both surprised to discover one another. More commonly, she and a half sibling discover one another. Sometimes, her half sibling was raised by their biological father, and other times neither she nor her half sibling have any idea who he is.

MAKING CONTACT

When you initiate contact with the adoptee or person with unknown parentage via the DNA testing company's email feature, be friendly and brief. Introduce yourself and the fact that you noticed him among your DNA matches and express your desire to be in touch. If he is not your child, let him know you noticed him among your DNA matches and that you'd like to be in touch to discover your connection. Do this in your own words and be sure to provide your email address and phone number, letting him know you welcome an email or call. State your preference, your time zone, and the best way and time for him to reach you. Then comes the hard part: Be patient.

If you receive a response immediately and his tone is enthusiastic and joyful, you'll know more how to proceed. If you don't hear back from him within a few days, it doesn't necessarily mean that he is not receptive. It's possible he's been busy, tested as a hobby and hasn't had a chance to log in to his account or email or to respond.

Allow a few days for a reply. If you haven't heard back in a week, reach out again. The frustration of delay motivates some to write very lengthy messages about who they are, who he is to them (or who they think he is to them) and every emotion they are feeling about it, as if they already know or are in contact with him. I strongly encourage you to refrain from doing this. Understand that he may already be overwhelmed, and such a message may scare him off. Also, some things are better said on the phone, after you know he is agreeable to contact, especially because the topic is a delicate one. Consider, too, that nowadays we can't be certain who else may be privy to another person's messages.

If he invites you to call him, ask when the best time may be for him to speak privately and without interruptions. The latter part is key, as interruptions can cause people to hang up prematurely, which can create feelings of upset or rejection in the caller. The very nature of the conversation makes it an emotionally charged one for both parties, even if it doesn't begin that way.

Sometimes the adoptee requires emotional space to process his feelings and come around. Going slowly is sometimes the fastest way to the best possible outcome for all involved. So, if you haven't heard from him after reaching out twice, wait at least two weeks before sending another message, which should be positive, brief, and indicating your hope of a reply when they have the chance. Mark your calendar and go about your life. Contact is what happens when you're busy doing other things.

I've offered this sound and conservative approach to help ensure the best possible first contact between you.

THE FIRST PHONE CALL

When preparing for their first phone call, both parties are nervous and a bit stressed. Some want to rehearse what they will say, fearful of communication missteps. They feel as though they have one chance to get it right and the possibility of what they want most, namely a reunion in person and an ongoing relationship, is riding on the success of the first conversation. It's do-or-die—and they are tongue-tied.

Prior to their first call, people often ask, "What do I say? How do I begin?" Both parties want to be well-received and viewed in the best possible light by the other. They listen for my answer, sometimes with pen in hand, and I respond, "Say hello!" This usually sparks a laugh. The idea is to get them to relax, and laughter is some of the best medicine for that and for reducing stress (and cortisol levels).

I encourage both parties to be themselves and suggest they not overwhelm the other with too many questions on the first call. There will be plenty of time for that later. Take it *slow*. Pay attention to the tone of the other's voice, pace, and emotions and respond accordingly.

Sometimes just saying, "I'm so nervous," or "I have no idea where to begin," is a great ice-breaker that makes both parties laugh and relax, knowing they already have something in common.

"Me too!" the other usually responds. When both parties are able to unburden themselves by expressing what they're feeling, it enables them to start breathing again . . . and then, they're *off to the races*.

INTERMEDIARY SERVICES

If you are not comfortable reaching out directly or have attempted contact to no avail, I also provide the service of acting as intermediary on behalf of adoptees' biological family members. I can be reached via the "contact" form, on my website (www.geneticgenealogycoach.com).

10

Downloading Your Raw DNA Data and Uploading it to Other Sites

DOWNLOADING YOUR RAW DNA DATA FROM ANCESTRY

STEP	ACTION
1	Log in to your AncestryDNA account at Ancestry.com.
2	Click on "DNA" in the main navigation bar. **Result:** *Drop-down menu appears.*
3	Click on the first drop-down menu item: "Your DNA Results Summary." **Result:** *The Summary page opens.*
4	In the large gray header, where it says "Hello…" (followed by your name) click on the "Settings" button, in the upper right-hand corner. **Result:** *The "Test Settings" page opens.*

Ancestry

5	Scroll down to the bottom of the page to the "Actions" box. Notice "Download Raw DNA Data," and click on the "Download" link (to the right) to initiate your raw DNA data download. **Result:** *You will be prompted to enter your Ancestry.com password and must check the box below, beside the terms:* *"I understand that after my DNA data is downloaded, the downloaded copy will not be protected by AncestryDNA's security measures. When I download my raw DNA data, I assume all risk of storing, securing, and protecting my downloaded data."*
6	Check the box beside the downloading terms and then click the green "Confirm" button below. **Result:** *A message will appear:* *"Almost there . . .* *Please check your inbox for an email from us. Then follow the instructions to begin your download."* **Note:** This is an added security step to ensure your privacy.
7	*Check the email inbox of the email address associated with your Ancestry account, for an email from Ancestry.* *The subject header will read: "Your request to download AncestryDNA raw data. "* **Note:** It can take a few minutes (and sometimes as long as twenty-four hours) for the email to arrive.
8	Open the email from Ancestry. In the body of the email, click on the large blue button that says, "Confirm Data Download." (You may be prompted to re-enter your password; if so, enter it.) **Result:** *The Ancestry window "Download DNA Raw Data" will appear.*

9	Click the green button (single click) that says, "Download DNA Raw Data," and do not close the browser window. **Result:** *The file is a Zip folder that will download to your hard drive.* **Note:** The Zip folder will be named "dna-data-..." followed by the date. **Example:** "dna-data-2020-09-01.zip" You may change the file name, but do not change the ".zip" file extension.
10	Locate the Zip folder on your hard drive. (Open your computer's File Explorer and locate the Zip folder. It may automatically download to your "Downloads" folder.) **Note:** DO NOT open or extract files from the Zip folder, as you will be uploading this folder, intact, to the other DNA websites. **Tip:** Move the Zip folder file to your computer's Desktop (or other location) where you will be able to locate it easily during the process of uploading it to the other DNA websites.

Ancestry

UPLOADING YOUR RAW DNA DATA TO FamilyTreeDNA

STEP	ACTION
1	Go to www.familytreedna.com.
2	Click "Upload DNA Data" from the main navigation bar on the home screen. **Result:** *Drop-down menu appears.*
3	Select the first item in the drop-down menu: "Autosomal DNA" **Result:** *The "Join Today" page opens, and you will be prompted to create an account.*
4	Get started for FREE by entering your name, email address and gender and click the orange "Join Today" button. **Result:** *The "Transfer Raw Data and Get Your Results" page opens. Also, you will receive TWO emails from FamilyTreeDNA; one with your system-generated "Kit Number" (which acts as your username) and a temporary Password.*
5	Select your transfer type by clicking on the appropriate button: **23andMe/Ancestry OR MyHeritage** **Note:** FamilyTreeDNA accepts raw DNA data uploads from three different DNA companies: 23andMe, Ancestry, and MyHeritage. If you have tested with more than one DNA company, select the transfer type relevant to the company's results (the raw DNA data file) that you have chosen to upload to FamilyTreeDNA. It is not necessary to repeat this process for each test taken; results from any one of those companies will do.
6	Click on "Browse file" and a window appears where you can select the file path and file itself and then click "Open." **Result:** *The file name will appear in the gray box.*

FamilyTreeDNA

7	Click the orange "Submit" button. **Result:** *A congratulations message box will appear containing your Kit Number and letting you know, "Your transfer has completed successfully."* Also, you will receive a THIRD email from FamilyTreeDNA letting you know that it will be three to five days before your results are ready. In this email, you will also be prompted to sign the release form.
8	Go to the email inbox associated with your FamilyTreeDNA account and open the third (most recent) email. In the body of the email, click the "Sign Release Form" button. **Result:** The "Consent to Participate in Matching" page will open. We want to consent to see our DNA matches (genetic relatives) list and to be seen in their matches lists. **Check the box beside:** "I agree to allow FTDNA to make my information available to a genetic match," and then click the orange "Continue" button.
9	Last, reset your Password. Click on your name in the upper right-hand corner and select "Account Settings" from the drop-down menu. **Result:** *The "Account Settings" page will open. (You may choose to complete profile information here, as well.)* Click on the "Password" link (to the right of "Contact Information," which is underscored in orange). Enter the current Temporary Password emailed to you from FamilyTreeDNA in the "Current Password" field and choose a new password, enter it in the space provided, confirm it by re-entering it in the space provided, and click the "Save" button. Be sure to write down your new password. **Result:** A message will appear: "Password has been updated." Also, you will receive an email from FamilyTreeDNA alerting you that your password has changed.

UPLOADING YOUR RAW DNA DATA TO MyHeritage

STEP	ACTION
1	Go to www.myheritage.com.
2	Scroll down to the footer, and under "Home," click on the link: "DNA." **Result:** *The DNA page opens.*
3	With your cursor, hover over "DNA" in the main navigation bar at the top of the screen. **Result:** *Drop-down menu appears.*
4	Click on "Upload DNA Data." **Result:** *The "Upload DNA Data" page opens.*
5	Click the purple "Start" button. **Result:** *You will be prompted to create your FREE account on MyHeritage.*
6	In the form provided, enter your gender, name, email address, and a password and check the box agreeing to the Terms of Service and Privacy, then click "Go." Be sure to write down your password. **Result:** *The "Upload DNA Data" page opens.*
7	In the gray box, check all three boxes (indicating whose DNA you are uploading and agreeing to the terms of the site) and then click the purple "Upload" button. **Result:** *A window appears where you can select the file path and file itself and then click "Open." Your data will automatically upload. When the upload is complete, a message will appear: DNA uploaded successfully."* *Click the "Done" button and log out.*

MyHeritage

UPLOADING YOUR RAW DNA DATA TO GEDmatch

STEP	ACTION
1	Go to www.gedmatch.com.
2	Scroll to the bottom of the homepage and see, "Not Registered? Click HERE." Click on the word "HERE." **Result:** *The "User Registration" page opens.*
3	Enter your name (it is preferable to use your real name), email address, and password and click the "Register" button. **Result:** *A message appears saying that an email has been sent to you with a "registration confirmation code."*
4	Leave the current GEDmatch window open and in a new window, go to your email inbox. Open the email from GEDmatch, copy the registration confirmation code, and paste it in the space provided on GEDmatch. Then click the "Confirm" button. **Result:** *A message appears: "Successfully Registered."*
5	Click the Log-in button in the upper right-hand corner of the page. Enter your email address and password and then click the "Log In" button.
6	Read the terms of service and privacy policy. At the bottom of the page, under option 1, click the designated link to accept GEDmatch's terms. (You will not be able to use the site without accepting the terms). **Result:** *A message box appears: "Hi There!"* *Click the green "Let's upload my DNA data!" button.* **Result:** *You are returned to the GEDmatch homepage and a bubble appears: "Great! Go ahead and click here to be taken to the DNA data upload page."*

GEDmatch

7	Click on the link: "Generic Uploads (23andMe, FTDNA, AncestryDNA, 23andMe)" **Result:** *The "GEDmatch raw DNA upload utility" page opens.*
8	On the "GEDmatch raw DNA upload utility" page, enter your name, gender, and the name of the testing company, and specify whose DNA you are uploading (example: Your DNA). Select a privacy option (default "Opt-in" is recommended) and click the "Choose File" button. (If your maternal and/or paternal haplogroups are known, you may enter those, too).
9	Click the "Choose file" button immediately beneath the privacy options, and a window appears allowing you to select the file path and file itself; do so and then click "Open." **Result:** *The file name will appear to the right of the "Choose File" button.*
10	Click the "Upload" button to the right of the file name. **Result:** *The "Upload" page opens.* *Check the box beside "I am not a robot," and your upload will begin. (You may be prompted to enter a captcha code in order to continue).* **Note:** Leave window open until uploading process is complete. An "Assigned Kit Number" will appear toward the bottom of the page when it's complete. Write down your Kit Number and close the program.

DOWNLOADING YOUR RAW DNA DATA FROM 23andMe

STEP	ACTION
1	Log in to your 23andMe account at www.23andme.com. **Result:** *Drop-down menu appears.*
2	Click on "Browse Raw Data." **Result:** *The "Your Raw Data" page opens.*
3	Click the "Download" link located beneath the main navigation bar. **Result:** *The "Download Raw Data" page opens.*
4	Scroll down to the "Request raw data download" portion of the page. Check the box beside: "I understand the limitations and risks associated with uploading my information to third-party sites." Click the blue "Submit Request" button below. **Result:** *A message appears: "Your download request is in progress."*
5	Check the email inbox of the email address associated with your Ancestry account for an email from 23andMe. The subject header will read: "Your 23andMe raw data download is ready!" **Note:** This is an added security step to ensure your privacy.
6	Open the email from 23andMe, and in the body of the email, click on the large green button that says, "Download Raw Data." (You will be prompted to log in again. Do so.) **Result:** *The "Download Raw Data" page opens.*

23andMe

	7	Click the blue button (single click) that says, "Download Raw Data," and do not close the browser window. **Result:** *A small window will open, prompting you to either open or SAVE the file (Zip folder).*
	8	Select the "Save File" option and click "OK." *Result: Another window will open in which you can select a file path and save the file.* Select the desired file path to save your Zip folder to and click "Save." **Result:** *The Zip folder will download to your hard drive, in the chosen location.* **Note:** The Zip folder will be named: "genome . . ." followed by your name, the version number of the test, and the date and transaction number. **Example:** "genome_John_Doe_v4_Full_2020 090123456.zip You may change the file name, but do not change the ".zip" file extension. **Note:** DO NOT open or extract files from the Zip folder, as you will be uploading this folder, intact, to the other DNA websites.

Sometimes the various DNA testing companies and utilities change their downloading and/or uploading instructions. Be sure to visit my website (www.geneticgenealogycoach.com) for the most current instructions on how to download and upload your raw DNA data. I often perform these actions on behalf of my clients or walk them through the processes in real time.

PART 5

Case Studies

11
Search Outcomes

A doptees and others with unknown parentage frequently ask about my search and others' searches, hoping or believing that knowledge will give them an idea of how long their search will take and how they might be received by the people in their own families of origin. I often respond, "I could write a book about all the searches I've done, and it wouldn't help the next person answer those questions. The outcomes are as different as the people they involve."

They often reply, "You should!"

They are interested in hearing others' stories. They find it comforting to know that many others have experienced the same feelings, and they want to know how others' journeys have played out, particularly those that are similar to their own. Some find that others' stories provide them with a feeling of emotional preparedness for what the future may bring. I know I did when I was searching.

For adoptees and others with unknown parentage, the journey of DNA testing and awaiting results is filled with emotions that range from joyful anticipation to fear of rejection. Many adoptees' searches began long ago, before DNA testing was available, and already include the emotional highs and lows, twists and turns, roadblocks and epiphanies, joys and frustrations that all great and worthwhile journeys involve.

Discovering the truth of your origins is only one part of the journey, and it is wise to be prepared for any number of search outcomes. The following are some of the possibilities:

- One or both of your birth parents may or may not be receptive to contact. It is important to note that of the cases I have worked, over 95 percent of birth mothers are receptive and interested in making contact and developing a relationship with the child(ren) they placed for adoption.

- One or both of your birth parents may have passed away. You may learn that one passed from a terminal illness to which you may or may not be genetically predisposed. Family medical information can literally save your life. I recommend that all female adoptees test to see if they have inherited mutated BRCA-1 and BRCA-2 genes, which pose increased risk for breast, ovarian, and other cancers.

- One or both of your birth parents may have a physical or mental disability due to an accident, age, or genetics.

- One or both of your birth parents may have been over or under the age of legal majority at the time of your birth.

- One or both of your birth parents may have been unwed, married, separated, or divorced at the time of your conception or birth.

- Nonidentifying information about one or both of your birth parents may prove to be true, partially true, or completely false.

- You may have full siblings; this is not common, however some birth parents later marry one another and go on to have other children, and some birth mothers surrender more than one child, by the same father, for adoption.

- You may or may not have any half siblings.

- Some of your siblings may be overjoyed to learn of your existence, while others may need time to process their feelings and share the new information with other family members before being in touch.

- Some siblings refuse contact and come around later, while others never come around, sometimes displacing their anger toward their mother (for keeping the sibling a secret) or their father (for having had an affair that produced a child) or for other reasons.

- You may be welcomed into the family right away, with open arms. But it is wise to be prepared to give genetic family members some time and space to go through their own emotional process and to be willing to slowly nurture those relationships. Sometimes the relationships we hoped for are not possible and/or do not materialize as hoped.

- The "honeymoon period" with genetic family members may last weeks, months, or years. Eventually, you may be treated like every other member of the family, and that may or may not be a good thing.

- You and/or members of your families of origin may ultimately end up feeling as if you have always known and loved one another and enjoy a good relationship. And sometimes even under those circumstances, it is possible to have a falling out and no longer be in contact.

The list goes on and could literally fill another book. The stories I have chosen to include here provide a glimpse into the real-life experiences of truth seekers.

It is my intent, and that of those who contributed their stories, to inspire and encourage you on your journey and to prepare you for what you may experience along the way. I appreciate their generosity of spirit and inclination to want to help others and thank them for doing so, as well as for their kind words regarding their experience working with me. Their stories and photos can also be seen on my website: www.genet-icgenealogycoach.com.

IN THEIR OWN WORDS...

Verne Albright, Canada

When Gerri Berger was recommended to me, I had been searching for my birth mother for over thirty years. My biological father and the mother who raised me (his wife) were both deceased, and all I had was the "mother's name" on my birth certificate. I hadn't been able to find a scrap of evidence that she existed, no birth or death certificate, no social security card, no marriage certificate, no record of employment or membership in a union, no mention in a newspaper . . . nothing. I had concluded that the name on my birth certificate was an alias, and I would never know my biological mother.

Poor Gerri! All I could give her was an alias. As it turns out, the name my father knew her by was not her name at birth—not even close! And back when I was born in 1941, there were no DNA tests. In doing her analysis, Gerri had to work with people who were only distantly related to my mother.

Several professional genetic genealogists had declined to

take on the job, and others had asked a price far beyond my means. Gerri's services cost a fraction of theirs.

In less than a week, Gerri told me she was confident she'd found my birth mother and gave me a name. I was skeptical she could have solved this perplexing mystery in a week when I had been unable to make any progress in thirty years. But there is absolutely no doubt she found the right person. Unfortunately, my mother was deceased by then, but I now have delightful and rewarding relationships with two of her half brothers.

To give an idea of the enormity of the task I gave Gerri, I point to the fact that even with my mother's name and pedigree, I have never been able to find anyone who knew her—except one of my new uncles, who'd met her one time when he was seven years old.

Gerri has my highest possible recommendation for her genius, tireless determination, enthusiasm, reasonable rates, and helpfulness while I searched for someone who knew my mother, and for the way she has remained a close friend in the years since she made my "impossible dream" come true.

Kris Burke, Illinois

I found Gerri through the ALMA registry when I started my search in 2017. I had done my AncestryDNA test, a 23andMe test and FamilyTreeDNA. I was in search of my birth parents.

When I got my ancestry DNA results, I had two first-cousin matches and three second-cousin matches, but I had no idea where to go from there. None of them had any idea who I could belong to. I contacted Gerri and she told me that with matches that close, she would be able to solve my case very quickly.

To my surprise, my DNA matches were on my father's side. Within just a few short days, I was put in touch with two half sisters on my father's side. I have gotten very close with one of my sisters.

Through the Salvation Army, I was also able to receive my nonidentifying information and was able to figure out the identity of my biological mother. Gerri was willing to contact her for me also.

Even though it seems that neither biological parent wishes to have contact at this time, I have been embraced by other family members.

I can never repay Gerri for the happiness I've found in my new relatives! It means so much to finally have a biological connection and to be accepted by them. Gerri and I also have built a lifelong friendship, and I am eternally grateful for her. I highly recommend her!

Richard Cole, Georgia

In 1944, at the approximate age of two weeks, I was left behind in an Atlanta hotel room. After spending time in foster care, I was adopted and raised by two wonderful people, who will always be my mom and dad.

Although, from time to time, I wondered who my birth parents were, I didn't pursue the answer until long after Mom and Dad were deceased.

Curiosity and that little "Who am I" feeling finally motivated me to begin my search. Two years and two DNA tests later, all I had were second to fourth cousins; no close relatives. I gave up.

Four more years had slipped by when last year, a neighbor told me about a lady who helped her verify and extend her family tree. She highly recommended Gerri Berger and added that she specializes in cases of unknown parentage. I decided to give her a call, and I cannot tell you how glad I am that I made that call.

Gerri went to work, and I crossed my fingers. Well, Gerri didn't need good luck from crossed fingers. I soon learned she is very, very good at what she does. After being a mystery for seventy-four years, Gerri identified and located my birth parents.

Although they were both deceased, there was some exciting, good news. Both of my parents had children other than me, so I had siblings. Even better, all of them were still alive. Gerri made meeting my new siblings so easy. As she located each sibling she, with care and discretion, informed them of my existence and desire to meet them. Everyone was excited and anxious to meet me.

My wife and I decided to host a DNA dinner party and invited Gerri and the couple who referred her to celebrate the end of my lifelong wonderment. That evening, my wife told Gerri of a grandfather in her family tree that had unknown parentage. Gerri later solved her family mystery, too!

When one of my half sisters came to town with her husband for a weekend visit, we invited Gerri to lunch. Gerri has become a friend of our family, and it is clear to anyone who knows her that she is passionate about reuniting families. Thanks to Gerri, my wife and I just returned from a wonderful week of happy and long overdue family reunions . . . in Iowa!

As a little girl, I remember my dad and his siblings discussing who they thought their maternal grandfather was, my paternal great-grandfather. At the tender age of seven or so, I wondered why, if I knew who my daddy was, no one knew who Grandma's daddy was. This had been a family mystery but not something the family ever discussed. When I was twelve, to everyone's astonishment, my great-grandmother told me his name.

I have researched for decades who the man we thought my paternal grandmother's father was and even recently attended one of their family reunions. I recently discovered that their DNA did not match my family's DNA. This was perplexing and made me want to research further.

I was lucky to discover Gerri Berger and thought I would give her a call to see if I could learn the truth behind my grandmother's parentage.

Gerri was delightful! During my consultation, I told her my story, and we reviewed my DNA matches together. She let me know that she thought she could solve the case and would be happy to work with me.

To my delight, a couple of days later, Gerri left me a voicemail letting me know that she had discovered the identity of my paternal great-grandfather! I was literally shaking and could not wait to learn more.

With great enthusiasm, knowledge, and patience, Gerri walked me through her findings. I was fascinated, and as it turns out, I am the direct descendant of a Revolutionary War patriot and as such, a Daughter of the American Revolution! I feel very fortunate to have worked with Gerri, and my family and I are thrilled with all that I have learned from her research and invaluable expertise.

I was born in Philadelphia and raised in Connecticut by an amazing family. We lived in a wonderful neighborhood in a very nice, middle-class section of town.

I was told at a young age that I was adopted but didn't really understand what that meant as a child. I just knew I had so many more interests than most of all my local friends and family.

It was two years after my mother's passing when I fully understood the importance of knowing my own history and whether or not there were any family health issues. That's when I turned to the idea of taking a DNA test. My DNA results were delivered four weeks later, and WOW! I was completely overwhelmed . . . so much data and information to handle. This is when I knew I needed help! I joined a group on Facebook and within two hours I had been told about a woman who "solves adoption search cases and she is amazing . . . her name is Gerri Berger, she is an adoptee herself and a genetic genealogist who finds adoptees' birth parents."

Gerri changed my life completely within six weeks. Mine was a difficult case. Not only had she found my birth mother but also my birth father. It was so much fun working with Gerri as we put our heads together, at times, to make sense of clues. She made connections with people within both of my biological families as well as at funeral homes and cemeteries to gather information.

Her knowledge and ability had me in complete awe. She is truly one of the most wonderful people in the world, and I love her for all she has done for me and my family.

Gerri did a great job as intermediary, despite the fact

that each side of my family initially denied any involvement. About a month later, and after several conversations with birth parents, I packed up and headed to Texas, where both of my birth parents were from and where they still live. Not only did I meet my birth mother and half siblings . . . but I also met my biological father and more half siblings. We now are all reconnected and all so thankful to our true friend, Gerri. My four boys now have five new cousins who have all built relationships that will be lifelong. One of my uncles keeps asking when our "reunion angel," Gerri, is going to come out to the ranch for supper!

This would have never happened if it weren't for Gerri. She is truly a reunion angel, and I will forever be grateful, with a full heart of love and respect. Our Oklahoma family is now connected for life . . . all thanks to my sweet, dear friend.

Michael Fischer, New York

I have known I was adopted as far back as I can remember. My parents told me at a very young age that they brought me home shortly after my birth. My mother shared with me as I got older that she and my dad could not conceive. So, for her to adopt me was the most wonderful answer to her prayers, and I was truly her son. She always gave me unconditional love, and she was the best mother anyone could wish for!

When I became an adult and had children of my own. I became a little curious about my background and wondered if there was any medical history I should know about. My parents didn't know anything. I never really pursued this quest, as I was so happy to have grown up with such an amazing mother and father.

I met Gerri in the mid-1980s. We went to the same small

college in New England, where everyone quickly knew everyone. We became good friends and stayed in touch on and off over the years. I knew Gerri was adopted and found it amazing, her passion to reunite families of origin. On multiple occasions, she encouraged me to do a DNA test. I had just lost my mother, my father's health and memory were not good, a lot was going on, and I didn't feel the time was right. Gerri said that because of my age, I may want to consider testing sooner than later. She was concerned I would miss an opportunity to unite with relatives while they were alive. I heard what she said, but I was so preoccupied that I continued to postpone.

Months later, my wife gave me a DNA test kit as a Christmas gift. I reached out to Gerri, who immediately encouraged me to take the test and offered her expertise in doing the research. I retained Gerri to begin her work.

Within a short period of time, Gerri told me she had found my birth mother and was in communication with my half brother, who was interested in connecting. He and I talked on the phone for quite a while, and I learned that my biological mother had never shared her story about me with her family. Neither her husband nor her children knew anything of my existence. So, we have kept things at a distance, as my intentions were not to put any pressure on her but for her to know that I'm well and have a great life. If she wants to connect, that's fine.

During that conversation with my brother, Gerri was texting me and trying to call me. Finally, I realized that obviously something major was up, so I finished my conversation and called her.

Gerri had just found my birth dad, and he wanted to communicate right away! Gerri shared with me that my biological father had been searching for me for over fifty years on and off with no luck. He and my birth mother were from the Bronx and were sweet on each other in high school. My birth mother became pregnant and was sent to stay at an unwed mothers home to give birth in the final months of her pregnancy. My birth dad, who was only seventeen years old, went to visit her periodically. He told me about the first and last time he got to hold me in his arms and how it broke his heart to know he'd never see me again. He said he told his wife about me from the beginning of their relationship, and she was always supportive of his search for me. He never shared the story with his daughter because the chances were so slim of finding me. Well, now my half sister, who grew up as an only child, has a brother, and she could not be more excited!

Our reunion took place in Georgia, at my birth dad's home. He, his wife, his daughter, and his son-in-law could not have been more welcoming, loving, warm, and accepting. I was welcomed with open arms!

Sadly, my birth father passed away within a year of our reunion. I called Gerri to share the news. I literally was in tears as I thanked my old friend for pushing me to do the research work and DNA test. Without Gerri, I would never have had this amazing opportunity to find out where I came from. I see the physical resemblance to my birth dad and that part of the family! While my birth mother hasn't come around, I understand and respect her reasons. I am in touch with my half brother!

If you are in your forties, fifties, or even sixties, don't wait! I'm so glad I entrusted Gerri with the task that I considered impossible. My dear friend, who has such a deep passion because of her own firsthand experiences, gave me the missing parts of the story of my life. I have met wonderful people who were looking for me. My birth dad, who reached out to Gerri periodically, said, "You answered my prayers!" I'm eternally grateful for what Gerri has done for me and my biological family!

Tracey Fuller, Canada

I discovered Gerri by fluke . . . or as I quickly learned . . . by fate.

One Saturday night, I was searching for another AncestryDNA group on Facebook. Gerri's page appeared in my search results, and I asked to join the group. That same night, she contacted me. We made arrangements to speak the following Monday, and she agreed to take my case.

My situation was a bit different. I'm not an adoptee, but I am a child of an adoptee, and I live in Canada.

I'd suspected all my life that my father was adopted. This suspicion was further validated with my AncestryDNA results, where I had "close family" matches with two people I had no knowledge of, and there were many unknown individuals showing up in our "shared matches." These two people were actually siblings (I will call them Jane and John), who were trying to determine their own heritage, as their father was also an adoptee. We struggled to figure out our connection and were not very successful.

My dad passed away in 2018, and I was able to confirm that he was adopted. However, my province wouldn't release any birth parents' information until they would have reached the age of 101. Jane and John did have their father's birth parent's information, but that lead proved to be a dead end.

After speaking with Gerri that Monday, she contacted me on Wednesday of the same week and informed me that she had identified my dad's biological father. Wow! I was blown away with how fast she delivered results—in only two days.

It turns out that Jane and John's father was my dad's biological father. So Jane and John are my dad's half siblings and my half aunt and half uncle. Gerri was also able to determine the correct name of the biological father's birth father. The name Jane and John received was an alias, which wasn't uncommon back then. So Gerri worked on a double adoptee case in Canada and solved it so quickly!

I asked her to continue with my case to identify my dad's birth mother. Within a week, she had solved that mystery as well!

The biological grandmother is still unknown, but I will pursue that angle another time with full confidence that Gerri will deliver results again.

I'm happy to have my suspicions validated and to just *know*. My grandparents were absolutely amazing, and I was so blessed by their love. People would ask me why I wanted to know when I had wonderful grandparents. My quest was never about dishonoring our relationship, as I treasure my memories. I have never been able to articulate my reasons for wanting to know, but Gerri understood completely about living in the know.

In the summer, when some of the COVID-19 travel restrictions had been lifted, I met my two aunts and uncle . . . my father's half siblings. It was the highlight of my year! Out of the blue, they said they would like to meet me, so I met them halfway, as we live two hours apart by car.

My new uncle is married to my dad's half first cousin on the maternal side—that's wild! So interesting that I'm doubly related to their children! She had pictures of my bio grandmother and let me know my dad has two half brothers on the maternal side.

My new aunt reminded me of my dad, and I wasn't expecting that, but it felt very comforting, which may sound weird. I never really had closure from my dad's death, but I feel like developing a relationship with them all was meant to help me with that.

Gerri is absolutely wonderful to talk to and explains things very well. You will not be disappointed in utilizing her services. She provided me with family trees and linked them to my DNA account.

She is truly a rock star! An angel! I am eternally grateful to her for helping me navigate my ancestral journey. I'm happy I found her when I did, which is why I believe it was fate. My heart is full of awe and respect for all she does . . . this is her passion, and it shows. I hope to one day give her one big hug!

Peter Haywood, Colorado

Fantasizing about who my birth parents were had been a persistent theme in my life since I was a little kid. In the opening scene of the movie, *Flirting with Disaster*, starring Ben Stiller, we see the perspective of a little boy in a stroller, as he looks at the legs of various women walking by and wonders, "Are you my mother?" I've had these very same feelings, for a long, long time.

Over the years, I had made a number of feeble attempts (I realize this now) to find my birth parents. Operating with insufficient or incorrect information, hamstrung by primitive technology, and frustrated by the sealed birth records in the state where I was born, I made no progress in my search.

Then, around 2010, I learned via Facebook that a

childhood friend of mine was reunited with his birth mother. He was overjoyed. It was interesting to me for several reasons, not the least of which was that I had no idea that he was an adoptee. Obviously, I was curious enough to get in touch with him to chat about his adoption search, and that is when he mentioned Gerri. He had nothing but the highest praise for Gerri, who was not only a professional genetic genealogist, but a high school friend of his from our hometown. Naturally, I contacted Gerri through Facebook, and this is where the saga of my real adoption search began.

It would likely be very boring for me to discuss all of the intricate details of how the search was done. Suffice it to say that if I didn't have the help of an expert like Gerri, I'd still be searching. Gerri understands the intricate details of interpreting DNA information, has wide-ranging database search skills, and has an intimate knowledge of the attitudes and behaviors of young mothers who were faced with the prospect and reality of giving up their babies. Personally, I had none of these skills.

I need to give the highest possible praises to Gerri for her brilliance, dogged determination, and sheer, unrelenting enthusiasm in helping me finally find my birth parents! I use the phrase "helping me" very loosely. She basically did the whole thing. Something that I could not have done in a gazillion years.

Gerri gets the highest endorsement and most profound thanks from me for her tireless efforts!

Though my search is now over, my experience continues to unfold in terms of relationships and connections. And Gerri has become my lifelong friend.

I was told that I was adopted from day one. My adoptive parents never hid that from me. I always dreamed of finding my biological parents, and it wasn't for lack of love—it was for knowledge and the feeling of belonging to someone other than the people who raised me. I just never felt I belonged.

At age fourteen, I started to ask my adoptive parents questions they couldn't answer. When I turned sixteen, my aunt helped me by asking my adoptive mom questions on my behalf. My mom had no information other than a paper with some nonidentifying information that didn't truly help.

At age twenty, I drove to Dansville, New York, where I was born, to find answers and hit a brick wall. No one would help. No one wanted to answer the questions I had, including questions about my health history. I hired a private investigator. No luck...he even gave me my money back. I truly felt alone and helpless. I kept asking my adoptive dad harder questions, only because he knew of my adopted sister's biological parents. He kept telling me I had "a closed adoption," though he had seen my biological mother once, at the court house. At this point, I signed up with every reunion group I could.

Fast forward to November 2018. My husband knew my history and suggested that I take a DNA test, so I joined My Heritage. Still no luck—only third to fifth possible cousins. My husband took an AncestryDNA test in January 2019 and suggested I test there, too. I was very broken and beaten down. I was heading into my fifties knowing nothing about my roots, and my chances of finding living biological parents were getting slim. I reluctantly tried AncestryDNA and received a "close match," but that person wouldn't respond to my message.

I felt heartbroken again, but I kept reaching out, determined to find answers. I was in need of the truth of who I am. I placed myself out there on Facebook and on every digital reunion site I could find. Along came Gerri Berger, who saw one of my posts and asked me if I needed help. I was very skeptical after hitting the wall so many times and after so many search angels had gotten my hopes up and tried to help me but either couldn't help or disappeared.

Gerri and I got on the phone together, and she asked me about my search, gave me some background on herself, and asked me if I had DNA tested. I gave her my login information and within one hour—seriously—she called me back and said, "I found your biological father."

I cried for an hour. I had never felt such a sense of relief. Later, I set up a time to discuss whether she could find my biological mother. Within nine hours of that conversation, Gerri had found her.

I turned fifty getting to know my biological mother through FaceTime and speaking with my biological half sister and brother on the phone. They all live in Washington State. I have been accepted in more ways than one. I also have a cousin in New York whom I have become friends with. On my biological father's side, I have spoken to an aunt on the phone, and she has been welcoming as has her daughter.

My dreams finally came true just in time for my fiftieth birthday! I can't thank Gerri enough!

Skye McGraw, New York

I met Gerri by chance through an ex-boyfriend who wrote a song about my search for my birth mom called "Simple Piece of Paper." Gerri was touched when she heard it and contacted me. Now, before I give the details on my angel, Gerri, I'll give you a little back story.

I was adopted two times—both times to horrible adoptive families. I decided to leave at age fourteen and start my life. But I always had this hole in my heart that only my birth family could fill. I had never known them and needed to find them to be happy. I had literally tried everything to find them. Every door slammed in my face. But I decided to take a DNA test, and that is where my angel comes in.

Gerri literally worked almost nonstop on my case for about two weeks to figure out who my family was. When we finally found them, she not only gave me the information but made the first calls for me to ease the first contacts. I could have never filled that void if it wasn't for her. I just needed to know who they were. And I got ten times more than that!

My birth mom and me were reunited on the day of my thirtieth birthday. Saying *thank you* is just not enough to express my gratitude.

Heidi Slacks, California

I was born in Modesto, California in 1958 and adopted at two days old. I always knew I was adopted and never knew who my birth parents were.

In 1993 (and after my parents had passed away), I decided I wanted to know more about my biological family and their backgrounds. I found a photo of myself as a newborn among my parents' belongings and on the backside of the photo the name "Bowman" was scribbled. I wondered if this could be my birth mother's last name.

I later learned that an attorney friend of my adoptive father handled the private adoption. There were no records to be found, as he was also deceased. I joined ALMA in 1994, and unfortunately my birth mother was not registered.

In October 2013, I decided to try DNA testing and tested with AncestryDNA and 23andMe. I was interested in discovering my true ethnicities and learning whatever I could about any hereditary health issues for myself and my children. I was also tired of "adopted—no family health history." Years passed, and I was still unable to find my birth parents.

In July 2018, I joined a few adoptee groups on Facebook, including Gerri's group, the Genetic Genealogy Coach, and read a lot of posts about adoptees' reunions with their birth parents and other relatives. I received a few messages from other adoptees suggesting that I contact Gerri, stating that she was great at finding people and easy to work with.

That was an understatement. She is fun and incredibly knowledgeable, loves what she does, and loves helping people. Gerri read my post in her group and messaged me, saying she would be glad to help me. We set up a call, and I asked Gerri to take on my search.

On August 17, 2018, Gerri messaged me that she had found my biological father and was waiting for confirmation on my birth mother and two half sisters! She went on to find more family members and built my very own family tree with my biological family on both sides, going back to the 1700s. This was all coming together within a little over a month!

After finding my family, a very large hole in my heart had been filled. At this point I was so happy to learn where I came from that it didn't even matter if I was going to meet any of them or not. I felt complete for the first time in my life, thanks to Gerri, and there are not words that can describe how grateful I am for the work and information that Gerri has provided to me.

I have since met my biological mother, two half sisters, a niece, two nephews, and my great-nephew on my mother's side. This year we spent our first Mother's Day with most of our new family. I have also met my aunt and two of her daughters and a great-aunt on my biological father's side. (He passed in 1987).

I still have more relatives to meet, and I have Gerri to thank every time I meet another family member. I would have never thought that I would feel so whole and complete now that my search is finally over.

Thank you, Gerri, for all your research, knowledge, coaching, suggestions, emotional support through the ups and downs, and your love and friendship. I would highly recommend Gerri for anyone searching for their family.

Derek Wasser, Virginia

I was adopted out of foster care in June 1970 by a wonderful family. As I grew, I often wondered why I had blond hair and Mom and Dad had black hair. My mom told me I was adopted when I was about twelve years old. I had a great childhood and joined the military after high school. While going through the process, many different doctors would ask about my medical history, and my answer was always, "I don't know." This happened throughout my life, and I always said that *one day*, I was going to find my birth parents.

In May or June of 2019, I decided to take a DNA test. While waiting for the results, I asked my mother about my adoption, and she gave me all the information she had. My mother's words were, "Your birth mother was young and in an unwed mother's home, and she didn't have a choice." I started doing some chair research. I had my birth name, where

I was born, and which social services agency conducted the adoption. I am not a private investigator, but I know Google is . . . and nothing.

I joined ALMA and was contacted by Marie Anderson. She is a great person and helped me get excited about the DNA results. When my results came in, I had an aunt and over 1,200 distant matches. I messaged my aunt and explained my story, and she said that she has three brothers. I thought, "Great! Who needs others' help? I'm about to crack the case!"

My aunt said that two of her brothers were deceased and had no children and the one who was living was not well and was not living in the area at that time. So, I had two possible dead fathers and over 1,200 distant cousins.

It was recommended that I call Gerri to review my findings, and at about 9:00 p.m. on a Friday night, we gave Gerri the go ahead. I went to sleep and wondered how long the search would take.

By Sunday, Gerri had sent me a message. "I found your birth mother." Holy sh**! I had every emotion running through me.

The next time we spoke on the phone, Gerri told me my birth mother's relatives and where they lived. Holy moly . . . one lived two miles from me! So, after we hung up, I got in the car and decided to become a "door knocker." (Gerri told me that this is called "door-stepping" and is not advisable, but I had to go.) I met a very nice lady (my birth mother's former sister-in-law). She called her brother (my birth mother's ex-husband) and later told me that I have two half siblings.

When I got home, I decided to call my birth mother (even though I'd asked Gerri to call) and oh boy! Not good! The last thing I heard her say was not to call *her* mother (my maternal grandmother, who is in her nineties). I called Gerri, and she calmed me down and asked if I wanted her to call. I agreed.

When Gerri called, my birth mother asked, "Are you calling on behalf of the whack job who is saying I'm his mother?"

Gerri left her contact info with her (and mine), for when and if she was ready to make contact. She was running scared and contacted everyone in her family to warn them of me and to say that what I was claiming wasn't true.

While waiting for Gerri to call me back, I got a call from the West Coast. A gentleman introduced himself as my birth mother's brother, and we discussed what was going on. I told him all I knew, and to my surprise, he told me that his father had told him the same story two months before he died. He said that my birth mother had just called him, denying the truth, and added, "Your birth mother doesn't know that I know." My uncle has been great to talk to, and he eventually told my birth mother that he knew the truth. To his (and my) surprise, she was relieved and told him everything.

Gerri had prepared me for potential outcomes and encouraged me to be patient, but it was still hard to bear her denial, which Gerri said was a "reflex reaction."

Since then, my birth mother and I have been in touch via email ("to establish a comfort level," she said), and I hope to meet her in person in the future.

I enjoyed working with Gerri and highly recommend her to other adoptees in search of their birth parents.

Acknowledgments

I would like to thank the following people from the bottom of my heart:

Leonard Berger, MD, my father, for your unwavering unconditional love. You continue to be the most wonderful father anyone could ever hope for and I feel like the luckiest girl in the world that you are my dad.

Gordon M. Berger (my brother), Patricia S. Singletary (his wife), Bryan A. Berger and Meredith E. Berger (their children) and our extended family (on both parents' sides), whom have been m family my whole life and could not be more a part of me if we were related by blood.

My birth mother, for your love and open arms. Our reunion healed me in ways nothing else could have. I would have searched for you forever and I'm forever grateful for you.

Rohana Contessa, my sister, for being the first to share our ancestry with me and encouraging me to write this book. And our siblings—Hass Contessa, Ib Contessa, Farlan Contessa, Sjarief Contessa, Nini Lettner, their spouses and children and our extended family, for your love and acceptance.

Louis Mangione, my uncle, for your love and for sharing our family history with me.

Marie Anderson of ALMA and author of this book's foreword, for your many years of friendship and dedicated service, caring, and contributions in the adoption search community.

Geraldine Brown-Giomblanco, my dear friend and author of Geraldina and the Compass Rose, for helping me navigate the waters of publishing my first book and for introducing me to Michelle Argyle and Kimberly Caldwell-Steffen.

My dear friends and relatives who have been a part of my journey to living in the know: BetteJo Andolino-Becker, Sheryl Bialo, Koren Borges, Marie Borowski, John Arnold Byram, Katherine Calich, Patty Callan Collings, Melinda Castriota-Avellino, Carol Chandler, Sue B. Christiansen, Ardienne Damicis, Nancy Davis-Lewis, Joan Edelman, Dolly Feldman, Paul Gadbois, Matthew L. Galfund, Deborah Gruberg-Smith, Dawn Guevares, Jonathan Hughes, Rachel Hulen-Pici, Jeanie Jackson, Jenny Johnsson, Diane LeVierge, Mary Macaskill-Cannon, Patricia Maio, Maria Mangione, Donna Mannino-Anderson, Scott Mascari, Marlene McDerment, Pamela McHugh-Klivan, Anna Misuraca, Pietro Misuraca, Christine Mueller-Milazzo, Sandy Musser, Janine Myung Ja, Anne Noonan, Kelly Noonan, Judy Perry, Richard N. Jr. and Jane H. Platt, Ellen Ribner-Guttierez, Beth Riccioli-Handy, Mene Roming, Chirlaine Santos, Levana Saxon, Linda Schiller-Egles, Abe Schy, Mia Schy, Steve Schy, Teresa Mangione-Schy, Joe Soll, John F. Trauth, Steven Vantine, Marina Vigna-Gigler, Linda Walls-Beauregard, Donna Williams-Segelquist, Anne Wolf, Jenette Yamamoto, and many others. You know who you are.

My former clients and dear friends: Verne Albright, Kris Burke, Richard Cole, Arnika Dawkins, Chip Evans, Michael

Fischer, Tracy Fuller, Peter Haywood, Janelle M. Lang, Skye McGraw, Heidi Slacks, and Derek Wasser for contributing your stories and kind words about your experiences working with me. And to the many others, too many to mention here, with whom I have worked and continue to hear from; your stories continue to inspire me and others. Thank you for allowing me to be a part of your journeys and for your referrals.

My publishing team of incredibly talented women, each of whom have honed their craft into an art form and made this book more than it ever could have been without them. I'm in awe. Thank you:

Michelle Argyle of Melissa Williams Design (book designer), https://mwbookdesign.com, for guiding me in the publishing process, making it smooth and seamless and for bringing this book from our collective computers out into the world, in print and e-book formats.

Kimberly Caldwell-Steffen (editor), www.kimberlyAcaldwell. com, the person who taught me that writing is rewriting—and that she is infinitely better at it than I am. Kim, you're an amazing listener and helped me achieve all I had hoped to in this book. I've enjoyed every moment of working together and couldn't have done it without you!

Erin Seaward-Hiatt (cover designer), www.erinhiatt.com, for your vision, creativity, patience, and revisions. We did it!

Last but not least, Stephen D. Yale, for your inspiration, collaboration, and being there every step of the way. I love you.

Bibliography

Berger, Geraldine. "Colorado: Access to OBCs and Non-ID." The Genetic Genealogy Coach. Accessed March 3, 2021. https://www.geneticgenealogycoach.com/adoptee-colorado-obc.

Berger, Geraldine. "New Jersey: Access to OBCs and Non-ID." The Genetic Genealogy Coach. Accessed March 1, 2021. https://www.geneticgenealogycoach.com/adoptee-new-jersey-obc.

"Birth Certificate." Wikipedia. Accessed February 20, 2021. https://en.wikipedia.org/wiki/Birth_certificate.

Brady, Adam. "8 Traits of a Spiritual Warrior to Help You Combat Avidya." Chopra. Accessed March 1, 2021. https://chopra.com/articles/8-traits-of-a-spiritual-warrior-to-help-you-combat-avidya.

Declaration of Independence, the. July 4, 1776. Accessed February 20, 2021. http://www.ushistory.org/declaration/document/.

"The Idea of Adoption: An Inquiry into the History of Adult Adoptee Access to Birth Records." Rutgers Law Review 53, no. 367 (2001). http://www.americanadoptioncongress.org/pdf/idea_of_adoption.pdf.

"Legitimacy (family law)." Wikipedia. Accessed February 20, 2021. https://en.wikipedia.org/wiki/Legitimacy_(family_law).

"Sexual revolution in 1960s United States." Wikipedia. Accessed March 1, 2021. https://en.wikipedia.org/wiki/Sexual_revolution_in_1960s_United_States#:~:text=With%20its%20roots%20in%20the%20first%20perceived%20sexual,were%20all%20important%20components%20and%20facilitators%20of%20change.

"Sexual Revolution of the 1920s." 1920swoman. Accessed March 1, 2021. https://1920swoman.wordpress.com/2011/05/01/sexual-revolution-of-the-1920s/.

About the Author

Geraldine Berger, known as the "Genetic Genealogy Coach," is a professional genetic genealogist, specializing in helping adult adoptees and others with unknown parentage to identify and locate their birth parents and other long-lost family members via DNA testing. In addition, she accepts traditional family-tree research projects and breaks though brick walls using DNA evidence.

A reunited adoptee herself, Gerri has solved hundreds of cases of unknown parentage as well as other family tree mysteries, including having identified her own biological father. She is an experienced intermediary between adoptees and their biological family members. Some of her successes have been documented in Sunday newspaper lifestyle sections and appeared on worldwide online news outlets. As an adoptee rights activist, she is a contributing writer for various media.

A dynamic public speaker, Gerri lectures on the topic of genetic genealogy at historical and genealogical societies, libraries, and other organizations. She earned a certificate in genealogical research from Boston University and has a master's degree in psychology from Fairleigh Dickinson University.

Gerri resides in Warwick, Rhode Island, and is a member of several national and local historical and genealogical societies, including the Daughters of the American Revolution (NSDAR) and the General Society of Mayflower Descendants (GSMD).

CPSIA information can be obtained
at www.ICGtesting.com
Printed in the USA
BVHW081335010721
610979BV00005B/61